Savvy

W⬤MEN

REVVING UP FOR
SUCCESS

Savvy Women
Revving Up for Success

"This is not just another book on success! Yes, it's fun to read, easy to comprehend, and simple to apply the principles found in its pages, but it also inspires action! And after all, action is where you find real power. *Savvy Women Revving Up for Success* harnesses the power that high-achieving women have used to grow their lives and businesses with significance during our new relationship economy. This book should be mandatory reading for all women, and for any man who knows a woman."
~ **Larry Broughton**, Founder & CEO broughtonHOTELS.com and yoogozi.com, Former US Army Special Forces Operator, Bestselling Author, Keynote Speaker

"If you've experienced failures or setbacks that prevented you from reaching your goals, then you are sure to be inspired by these women! *Savvy Women Revving Up for Success* includes twenty powerful stories from women who refused to give up in spite of their challenges and struggles. Reading these stories will remind you to get recommitted to your dreams!"
~ **Ursula Mentjes**, Two-Time Bestselling and Award-Winning Author of *Selling with Intention, One Great Goal* and *Selling with Synchronicity*

"Claudia Cooley has done an amazing job of capturing truly passionate stories that will not just encourage and uplift those who read *Savvy Women Revving Up for Success*, but will inspire them to go out and make a difference in their own lives and the lives of those around them."
~ **Kyle Wilson**, Founder of Jim Rohn Int and LessonsFromNetword.com, Author of *52 Lessons I Learned from Jim Rohn and Other Great Legends I Promoted* and Co-Author of *Chicken Soup for the Entrepreneur's Soul*

"We all need inspiration from those who have traveled the journey of pain, struggles, trials and tribulations. *Savvy Women* are here to help us move out from duress and into success. They share their stories and give hope and healing to those who need some motivation to create a new life chapter. Why go at life alone? Women need women. We lift each other up and encourage one another to keep on keeping on. Without some of these women in this book, my life would not be what it is today. Claudia's joy, compassion and love is contagious. She is truly authentic and at peace with who she is. But, more importantly, she loves mankind and wants to lift people up from their pain."

~ **Tanya Brown**, #1 Bestselling Author of *Finding Peace Amid the Chaos*, Life Strategist and Speaker

"Feel like giving up? Get inspired by the stories of the fabulous women in *Savvy Women Revving Up for Success,* you may find that your lucky break is just one day away! These women persevered in the face of adversity and dared to take the road of chance, and became empowered and successful because of it. Dare to go for it and design the career of your dreams!"

~ **Susie Augustin**, Bestselling Author of *Sexy, Fit & Fab Sirens* and *Sexy, Fit & Fab at Any Age!*

Savvy
WOMEN

REVVING UP FOR SUCCESS

Women Making a Difference in the World Today

CLAUDIA COOLEY

Published by:
Claudia Cooley Inc.
Grand Terrace, CA 92313
www.ClaudiaCooley.com

Limits of Liability and Disclaimer of Warranty
The author and publisher shall not be liable for your misuse of this material. This book is strictly for informational and educational purposes.

Warning – Disclaimer
The purpose of this book is to educate and entertain. The author and/or publisher do not guarantee that anyone following these techniques, suggestions, tips, ideas, or strategies will become successful. The author and/or publisher shall have neither liability nor responsibility to anyone with respect to anyone with respect to any loss or damage caused, or alleged to be caused, directly or indirectly by the information contained in this book.

ISBN 978-0-9856026-2-8 paperback
Library of Congress Cataloging-in-Publishing Data is available upon request.

Printed in the United States of America. First Printing, 2015

Editing by Get Branded Press www.GetBrandedPress.com
Cover & Interior Design by Kate Korniienko-Heidtman
Back Cover Photography (Claudia Cooley headshot) by Raul Lozano

Dedicated to all
Savvy Women Revving Up for Success
that are making a difference in the world.

I especially want to thank the women that said, "Yes!"
to sharing their stories in this book,
Inspiring others to see their own greatness and gifts inside
themselves as they continue to pay it forward.
We each make a difference.

I wrote this book for You.
We still have a lot to accomplish together in our world...
Our Legacy.

Acknowledgments

Like with each of my books, the people I meet ignite my creativity and need to share, including this one. The inspiration I receive from these amazing women prompted me to ask this question, "How do I bring these amazing women with their incredible stories of making a difference in big and small ways, to women that need encouragement and inspiration to experience their own greatness?"

It was a "God Wink" the day I was asking this question, and the idea for the book erupted in my head and heart and I just knew this was going to be a wonderful journey. So first and foremost, I want to give gratitude to God for His everloving kindness and what He has created in me, and for always showing me the way.

I want to thank my amazing husband for all of his support and for the numerous meals he prepared and cleaned up afterwards, to provide me the time to be dedicated to this journey. It would mean nothing without him. Our 50+ years together is my biggest treasure on earth.

To my amazing children and grandchildren, as they inspire me to continue toward my *Best Me*, Thank you. You are truly my treasures. To my dear friends that cheer me on faithfully - even though they call me a "Humming Bird" - they are such strong supporters.

And a huge *Thank You!* to my creative team.
Susie Augustin and Get Branded Press for hearing my first deepest desires for this book and supporting me with your energy and enthusiasm to make this possibility a reality. This journey has been ours together to honor these amazing women. Your dedication with time, resources and creative ability is so appreciated. Kate Korniienko-Heidtman for the stunning book cover creation and interior design, which captures the essence of the Savvy Women message. Rasheed Louis and Epiphany Marketing for sharing your authentic friendship, support and for bringing excellence to all of my projects.

CONTENTS

FOREWORD

This is the best time to celebrate women and the difference they are making in the world today. As the CEO of Women Network and President of the California Women's Conference, we are building a global community. I have a true and deep passion to inspire women to create opportunities to work together to affect our world and make an impact for the better...I really believe we are better together.

The wonderful book you hold in your hands shines a light on 20 women that are willing to be transparent as they share their stories of triumph over adversity, victory from struggle, and beauty from ashes as they each move forward with passion to give back to others and to make a difference powerfully. Their stories are deeply touching, full of honesty and the profound wisdom they discovered on the journey and now share with us.

You will be inspired to see your own greatness within and your possibilities to give to others. Your mind will open to new ways and paths to make a significant contribution to others in your family, community and the world. This is where true happiness and fulfillment are found.

Don't just read this inspiring book, but come and link arms with us to make our world better.

Women Network..Better Together!

Michelle Patterson
CEO of Women Network
President of the California Women's Conference
www.WomenNetwork.com

Michelle Patterson is the CEO of Women Network LLC, a media and production company giving women a voice to share their message. Women Network's "umbrella platform" shines a light on organizations and corporations who empower women and bring them together as a community to experience "We are Better Together." Women Network is creating the largest community of women globally. They are the exclusive event producer of the California Women's Conference. This fortunate relationship allows Women Network to provide additional promotional benefits to the California Women's Conference through its array of web media functions.

Michelle Patterson's name conjures up many credits – visionary, author, acceleration executive, founder, passionate, talk show host and dynamic speaker. She is a woman of many talents and dimensions. She is also the founder of Global Women Foundation, a 501 (c)(3) non-profit public charity created to bring women together to create global change by empowering them to transform their communities. Its mission supports women to effectuate this change through serving as a world-wide conduit for connecting community, mentoring, education, and financial support.

INTRODUCTION

"I have one life and one chance to make it count for something. My faith demands that I do whatever I can, wherever I am, whenever I can, for as long as I can with whatever I have to try to make a difference."

Jimmy Carter

Living life full out embraces who you are becoming as a person, and affects the differences you can make in the world and the lives around you. Over a lifetime I have experienced amazing mentors that showed up in my life and gave me inspiration, motivation and even sometimes a kick in the pants to reach for the best version of myself. Or as I like to say, to reach for my own personal A+ that is in me, and never to settle.

Mentors show up in many forms; as a person, from reading a book, or listening to CDs. Family members, friends or teachers may feed into who we are becoming. But I promise, *Balcony People* will show up, and it's our job to recognize and embrace what they offer as an amazing opportunity to become the person you truly are designed to be.

This book was inspired by the *Balcony People* concept. Those who are on their own journey of success and now *paying it forward* by reaching back and showing us how to miss the *potholes* and maneuver the *roadblocks* of life. *Savvy Women Revving Up for Success* includes 20 women inspiring us as they are making a difference. They may not even recognize their own gifts to the world, but their light shines for us to follow.

As you read these fascinating stories, you may find similarities in yourself. I find a bit of myself within each story. The goal of this book is for you to see the greatness in yourself, discover what gifts you are already sharing with others, and continue to grow by giving in a bigger and bolder way. As a former teacher, I realize if you can change a classroom, you can change a community, and if you change enough communities, you can change the world. We invite you to join us on this path.

HEALTH

Living Healthy is Living Life in Balance

Body • Mind • Spirit

HEALTH

*Living Life in Balance is like a dance…
find your rhythm, then create harmony
by moving to your own beat.*

Revving Up for Success and realizing successful outcomes require living a life in balance. This is where you find real fulfillment, happiness, fun, freedom and abundance. You will find a common thread in truly successful people and the women in this book - that living in gratitude overflows into contribution. It's in their truly authentic success that their giving back to the world flows from.

"Surprise Package" was my nickname when I was young. My parents had both been previously married and brought grown children into their marriage. My Mother had been told she wouldn't be able to have any more children. Imagine the total shock as they were informed of the upcoming event - my birth. Mom made some real sacrifices to ensure I arrived safely, by spending the last six weeks of her pregnancy in bed. My arrival was a celebration in our family, and I sensed that growing up. I knew I was loved.

My Daddy was my best friend. I became his sidekick and went everywhere with him. From very early on, every Saturday morning he woke me up and off we went to Fairmont Park Lake to fish. We prepared the night before by digging up the worms for our adventure. I learned quickly how to get the worm on the hook with what I thought was very little pain for the little worm. So on those early mornings as the sun came up and moved into the sky, I sat on the banks of the lake listening to Daddy's amazing stories. He shared his passion for people and for being a successful entrepreneur. He loved life and appreciated each moment.

During those amazing years I was filled with encouragement to step into who I could be, celebrate my possibilities, reach for the stars for I deserved them, and to always remember I was special. I realize I had a rich beginning and I live every day in gratitude for what my parents instilled in me. I developed a true belief in myself and for what I could accomplish if I set my mind to it and did the work.

Then one Saturday when I was eleven, Daddy returned home after traveling across country to be with his mother when she passed away. He'd only been home a few hours, when suddenly he died from a heart attack. He'd never been sick, but had always been overweight, such as was common on this side of my family. This was such a surprise; we just weren't prepared. I was there when this occurred, and I remember how overwhelmed my mom was. My older sisters, having their own homes and families to return to, told me I needed to be brave and to take care of Momma for she wasn't well.

I went to work when I was twelve to help support us. Daddy had so well prepared me on the banks of the lake, where he taught me about work ethics, making money, saving and careful spending. I could count money and roll coins before I ever went to school. So my very first job was working in a diner running the register, at age 12.

This story, my story, is why I'm so passionate about inspiring others to create a truly healthy living path; mentally, physically and spiritually. For almost four decades, I've been a teacher, coach, mentor, and hopefully an inspiration to empower individuals to live a life they love. This comes from living life in balance, what I call *Success Synergy*.

- Healthy Self-Confidence
- Healthy Body
- Healthy Spirit

To ignite our success in these areas, it takes intention and attention. Never ever take any of this for granted.

Who contributes to your *Healthy Self-Confidence?* Maybe it wasn't your family. That's ok. Go find your *Balcony People* I spoke of in the Introduction to this book. The people that stand up, cheer for you, and support what you are doing, who you want to be and are becoming. These are people you want to find and incorporate into your life, and my suggestion is to hold on to them tightly. One of my first *Balcony People* was my dad. The second was my husband; over 50 years of marriage and an amazing cheerleader. The third was Joanne Wallace, she saw I had more gifts than I even realized, mentored me, trained me then inspired me to step out and soar. For almost four decades, she remains in my life continuing to believe in me and cheering me on.

Healthy Body is an area we are able to decide only for ourselves. I like to ask my clients, *"Why* do you want to be healthy?" If their *"Why"* is big enough, they will achieve it. It truly is building healthy habits. For me, I've created really healthy eating habits, and now I work with determination to fall in love with exercise. Every day I set the intention. If I don't, it won't happen. So my suggestion is to eat right, drink tons of water, and create *activity* that increases your motion. Don't you love how I skirted the *"E"* word?

One of the most important areas that we need to fuel and often neglect is the *Healthy Spiritual* side of our design. For each of us, that will be different. For me it is my faith in God, and my spiritual journey is a daily walk in my belief. Prayer, meditation, journaling and then giving from that filled up place to others.

As I said in the beginning, *Revving Up For Success* and realizing successful outcomes require living a life in balance. This is where you find real fulfillment, happiness, fun, freedom and abundance. Now you have expanded your possibilities and truly will begin to make your difference in the world. And nothing makes life more *Juicy!*

HEALTH – BODY • MIND • SPIRIT

POWER WOMAN ENTREPRENEUR

by Kim Somers Egelsee

Many of us are confused as to how to get our life in balance, especially when we are trying to be superwomen. Overwhelm and stress can take over if we let it. Some of us get so caught up in daily life and what we should be doing, that it can become monotonous. It is important to decide to take control and believe that we can get every area of our lives in balance. It all begins with a commitment to work on yourself.

I was that woman. I was working hard as a special education teacher and liked it, especially the children, but I was not in my life's purpose. There was always that whisper of something else out there that was more aligned with my purpose, but I had not figured it out yet. Although I was a life coach for fun on the side, and had studied personal development for years, my life was a constant scurry of driving, doing paperwork, and being tired from the day. My job required heavy lifting with the children, so it would wear me out by evening. My life was out of balance, until one day I made a shift. I decided to leave teaching to focus on other things. I began to study coaching and other modalities, and stepped into my purpose as a life coach, speaker, author and confidence expert.

If you can say that you have harmony in all areas of your life, it is almost guaranteed that you will feel happy. This means that you know yourself. You have control over your ego and you're aligned with your life purpose. Having harmony keeps you open-minded and optimistic when working with others, doing business, and being creative. It means that even when stress or negativity enter your life, you can redefine it, work with it and still do well. To achieve this, start by making a list and rating everything important in your life on a scale from 1-10. For example, your love life may be at a 10, your finances at an 8, but your fitness and health at a 4. This allows you to see clearly the areas that need work.

The more I moved forward with action in my career as a life coach and speaker, asking for opportunities and creating my own, the more in harmony my life became. I constantly evaluated my life, removing the things that I was not fueled by. This activated more confidence in me because I was aligned with my power.

Getting your life to a 10+ and finding your purpose is possible for everyone. Simply follow the seven steps to a 10+ Life below.

The first step is to believe that it will happen. Focus on positive thoughts and banish all negative self-talk and beliefs. When negative thoughts come in, you can immediately imagine throwing them into the ocean. You can practice replacing them with positive thoughts. This communication to yourself and others can change your life for the better. To get the courage to step into my purpose and go for my dreams, I changed my thinking, communication and beliefs to positive. Any time negative words entered, I would throw them away.

The second step is to get in alignment with your purpose. If you're not sure what it is yet, you can state that your purpose is to become the best you possible by getting in line with your true self. Then, start remembering what you are passionate about. The realizations that you have are often your purpose. It helped me to realize my purpose when I made the space by leaving my teaching job. I also had more days available to be a life coach, and I knew I had found my calling.

The third step is to learn and grow. Join a mastermind group or find an accountability partner. Begin to read inspirational books, spend time with quality people, and attend seminars. The support system will elevate your success and motivate you to zoom forward fearlessly. My personal development studies helped me to step into what I am meant to do.

The fourth step is evaluating and identifying what needs changing. Women are not super heroes, although you often feel you are supposed to be. It is important to quit adding stuff to your schedule that you don't need, stop spending time with negative friends, and figure out what you need to remove, making the space for greatness to enter. This is a huge help with time management.

The fifth step is to seek those who can help you get to that next level of success with positive influence. Choose a regular group or event to attend monthly. The knowledge you gain and the people you meet can be priceless. After I left teaching, I began to search. I started to attend events with uplifting people, learning and growing. I asked for help and feedback with my plans.

The sixth step is goal setting. Make sure your goals are in line with your true self and word them positively. Schedule benchmarks toward each goal throughout your calendar. Most importantly, celebrate your successes. This reinforces in your mind that you are a successful person. To become a powerful entrepreneur, I knew I needed goals. I began thinking bold, and creating intention. Each time one of my goals was complete, I would do something to celebrate.

The seventh and most important step is value. Make sure that what you are regularly reading, where you are going, who you are spending time with, and what you are doing are matching that of which you see yourself becoming. Regularly check in with yourself. Be sure that you are taking action daily on getting your life to this high level of success, and soon you will realize, just like my story, that your life as a busy woman power entrepreneur has gotten to a 10+.

KIM SOMERS EGELSEE is the #1 Bestselling Author of *Getting Your Life to a 10 Plus: Tips and Tools for Finding Your Purpose, Being in Your Power and Living an Amazing Life.* She's a TEDx Speaker, a multi award-winning Confidence Expert, International Inspirational Speaker, Life Coach, Hypnotherapist, NLP Practitioner, TV Host and Columnist. She specializes in helping people get every area of their lives to a 10+ and exude confidence, connect authentically, and discover their life's purpose. Kim speaks at over 65 events, meetings and workshops per year. She's been very successful with her Ten Plus Life Coaching Certification Program and her collaboration on Claudia Cooley's Image Consultant Certification Program.

KIM'S *SAVVY WOMAN* TIPS

Check in with Yourself – At least four times per day, ask yourself, "What am I doing with my time, where am I going? How are my communication, attitude and behavior?"

Follow Your Passion – Do what fuels you, see and experience joy, adding energy to your life.

Make Sure all That You are Doing is 90-100% on Your List – Create a list of what you're doing presently in your life, and another list of your dreams and goals. Rate each item 0-100%. Make a conscious effort to focus only on the 90-100% items - you will sculpt your life by design.

Use Only Positive Communication – Try this for two weeks, and it can become a great habit and way of life that transforms everything.

Form a Mastermind with Your Top 5 – Make a list of the people that SUE you - **S**upport, **U**plift and **E**ncourage.

Find out more about Kim at
www.KimLifeCoach.com
www.KimsConfidenceCourse.com

HEALTH – BODY • MIND • SPIRIT

DIABETES DROVE ME TO MAKE LEMONADE FROM LEMONS

by Dr. Jody Stanislaw

It was June of 1980 when my gregarious and bubbly seven-year-old self took a dramatic downturn. I'll never forget it. I went from running around one day, to feeling listless and nauseous the next. Lying on the couch shockingly became more intriguing than going outside to play. My mouth was painfully dry. But no matter how much water I drank, my thirst was so intense it made me cry. My mom soon decided to take me to the doctor. After discovering my urine was full of sugar, I was immediately sent to the hospital. I was diagnosed with Type 1 Diabetes and my life has never been as carefree since.

Every single day in the past 34 years, I've poked my fingers multiple times a day and injected myself with the life-saving insulin, which my body no longer produces. I've had to monitor every bite of food I've ingested, and had to calculate how much insulin I need to keep my blood sugar level from dropping too dangerously low or high. There is no break from diabetes, unless I want to incur the devastating health complications caused by unregulated blood sugar levels.

Yet at the age of 41, I'm one of the healthiest women I know. I thank diabetes for this. I thank diabetes for motivating me to make healthy food choices. I thank diabetes for inspiring me to make exercise an integral part of my life. I thank diabetes for the strength and tenacity I have built from all the times I was struggling and wanted to give up, but didn't. I thank diabetes for my ability to relate and touch others who are struggling with intense physical or even emotional monsters. I thank diabetes for teaching me that I can conquer anything. I thank diabetes for driving me to always make lemonade when life hands me lemons. And finally, I thank diabetes for generating my passion to make a career out of helping others live healthier lives.

Spending that life-changing week in the hospital was when I decided exactly what I wanted to be when I grew up. The staff at Seattle's famous Children's Hospital was so joyful and friendly that they made what could have been the worst week of my childhood, one of the best. The most memorable part of that week was, astonishingly, how much fun I had. At the mere age of seven, I was so struck by this experience that it was then that I knew I wanted to become a doctor.

Yet, pursuing a childhood dream certainly wasn't all roses. Throughout my teens and twenties, the doctors I met during my checkups were far from the fun and inspiring ones I met back at the hospital. Most were unfriendly, stern, and did not seem to be helping anyone feel better, at least not me. Living with diabetes was often lonely and frustrating, and I rarely connected with anyone who really understood what I was going through. I dreamed of becoming the kind of heart-centered doctor I'd always hoped to find, but never could. I wanted to make a difference. But the intensity of medical school began to scare me; the demands of time, the investment of money, the rigors of studying. After meeting so many unhappy doctors, I doubted if going to medical school was an investment I really wanted to make. I was painfully torn since I'd spent my entire childhood dreaming of becoming a doctor.

This exasperating tennis match of to become or not to become a doctor played back and forth in my mind for over a decade. I tried to distract myself for a few years in my late twenties, when I entered pharmaceutical sales and attempted to convince myself that this alternate career was an easier and equally satisfying path to take. Yet, my deeper knowing was never convinced. I was selling the most popular antidepressant drug on the market, yet those five years were the most depressing years of my life. Then one auspicious day as I was sitting in a coffee shop, dreading having to make another sales call at a doctor's office, I happened to pick up a magazine featuring a story about a local medical school that was much more heart-centered than standard medical school. The curriculum focused on a whole person approach to healing that included nutrition, the benefits of exercise, herbs, meditation, mental wellbeing, and more. My smile beamed.

I immediately called the school and made an appointment to come out for a visit. They had an opening the very next day. I was thrilled. After my appointment, my decision was made. I soon quit my lucrative medical sales job at the age of 30 and took the plunge of entering medical school. Five intense years of study later, and almost 25 years after I had made the decision to become a doctor, I was finally announced as Dr. Jody Stanislaw. My desire to help as many people live healthy and happy lives is immense. Because of this, I have adopted a completely virtual medical practice business model, which allows me to interact with patients all over the country and world. Thousands of people receive my bimonthly Vitality Vibe email, full of simple and practical tips for living healthier lives. Hundreds of people have taken part in my group courses, and countless patients have had their lives dramatically improved after taking part in my three month E.A.S.Y. Lifestyle Transformation program.

Of course, I also specialize in working with fellow patients with Type 1 Diabetes. Being able to pass my life-changing wisdom for how to manage this disease so easily to others via phone or Skype, wisdom which took me decades of frustrating trials and tribulations to figure out on my own, is one of my greatest joys in life. After 34 years of living with what could be a devastating disease, yet being as healthy as I am, brings hope to every family with a child with Type 1, and to every patient feeling doomed by this disease. I am blessed to have the personal experience plus formal education, to lift patients out of their fears and to instill them with hope and inspiration. Thank you diabetes, for being the driving force behind my lifelong pursuit of bringing health and joy to thousands of people's lives. I feel blessed to take my lemons and make lemonade, not only for myself, but for hundreds throughout the world. Living with a chronic disease - my blessing in disguise.

DR. JODY STANISLAW is a Naturopathic Doctor, and earned her doctorate degree at Bastyr University, the nation's premier holistic medical school, located in Seattle, WA. While most medical visits only look to the problem at hand, Dr. Stanislaw has become an expert at helping patients build a strong foundation for good health through her Four Pillars of Health program. In this program, patients adopt skills for improving their nutrition, sleep, exercise, and emotional well-being. Given her desire to reach as many people as possible, she has an entirely virtual practice, allowing her to work with patients anywhere around the country via phone. She is also an author and speaker.

DR. JODY'S *SAVVY WOMAN* TIPS

Take Care of Your Body – When you feel good, you can conquer the world. When you don't, endless opportunities pass you by. You have one exciting life to live and the precious vehicle you have to carry you through this exciting ride called Your Life is your body.

See the Cup Half Full – Curve balls happen. The plans you have will fall apart. Rain will pour on your picnic. Your friend will forget to call you back. Your spouse will irritate you. But guess what? You're not alone. These things happen to everyone. These events are part of life.

Know What Makes You Happy and Make Time for It – This is your life. What kind of person do you want to be? What fills your heart with joy and satisfaction? Are you doing that? Make time for what makes you happy and boldly go for it.

Live by the 80/20 Rule – Perfection is a low expectation because it's impossible. It sucks up energy. The rule that I teach all of my patients to live by, and that I follow as well, is the 80/20 rule. Make healthy eating choices 80% of the time. Indulge 20% of the time. Let go of perfection.

Find out more about Dr. Jody at
www.DrJodyND.com

HEALTH – BODY • MIND • SPIRIT

COURAGE IS BEAUTIFUL

by Xiomara Escobar

One brisk afternoon in 1981, a woman two months pregnant with her first child was shopping for her weekly groceries in the open market in San Salvador, El Salvador. As she picked her oranges, she noticed what seemed to be a minor scuffle in the market corner. The skirmish, caught out of her peripheral vision, reminded her of the national curfew of five o'clock.

The political climate of her home was at a fever pitch. The government had declared martial law and now even in the capital, peaceful demonstration was no longer done in the main courtyard of downtown. The threat of severe physical harm and even death, were now very real consequences for political demonstration. She reminded herself of the days when she was a child, and how then El Salvador was a different country, concerned with just tourism, agriculture and education. Now its focus was held by its unstoppable plummet into civil war and which political party would be its victor. Civil unrest now spilled into violence in urban areas, and not just the rural towns. This violence included the deliberate terrorizing and targeting of civilians by death squads, the recruitment of child soldiers, and other violations of human rights, mostly by the military.

It was then in the woman's line of vision, that she saw a tank coming in towards the public market. Before she had a chance to scream, the first salvo was shot past her right side. She had to escape or likely die. She could run to the church where the bystanders were beginning to take refuge. However, not only were they closing the door to the church, bodies were piling up in ghoulish hurdles as the tanks were firing in that direction. The other choice was to get into a bus that was already moving out of the chaos on her left side, but still in harms way. She decided to run towards the bus, but as bullets started impacting towards its entrance, she had to claw her way through one of its windows to reach the salvation it offered. Adrenaline, prayers, and a growing mother's instinct pumped through her body and sprung her into this life preserving throe. When she finally made it inside the bus, she clung to the floor to avoid the continued and insatiable gunfire. It was there, surrounded by violence and death, that she promised herself that if she made it through the day, she would not raise her baby among this chaos. The bus driver gave a quick audible plea to God and then told everyone to hold on. She made it home alive and was greeted by her husband who had been desperately waiting for her return. When she saw him she gasped and cried in his arms, and together they both made a vow that their child was going to be born in a country of prosperity and hope. The decision my parents made that day resulted in me being born in the United States just seven months later.

So now if you ask me where I get my passion and drive, my answer is easy to give. My spirit is from those two courageous individuals that came to this country with only forty dollars to their name. My mother's courage did not end on that violent day in El Salvador. The challenges that she and my father faced once in the United States, continued to put obstacles that at times seemed insurmountable. They had no family or friends to rely on and could not speak English. Yet for me, as before, they found a way. As I grew up, I saw how my parents worked hard and achieved success because of their focus and commitment. They wanted their daughter to live in love and opportunity, and they would not be daunted by the difficulty of anything they faced. I was taken care of, but I also helped in the family business. I was taught early on that mom and dad were able to create financial independence through their work ethic and the passion they had for each other and their family.

After my days as a student at Chapman University, with a BS in Marketing, I had to make a name for myself. Like all journeys, it was tough and I had no idea what I was doing or where I was going. I am blessed that my Lord and Savior had a plan for me, and brought a beautiful Pink Sister in my life. I was introduced to my *Beauty World* filled with the knowledge and breakthrough of inner and outer beauty. I've enjoyed a career with Mary Kay for the past 6 years. I've been a Star Consultant over 14 times. I volunteer at the Domestic Violence Shelter in Orange at Casa Teresa and love to see a smile on a woman's face when she realizes her potential of being the woman God created her to be.

I had been praying about different ways to minister to others and I thought I had to go outside of the USA to make a difference until I started to volunteer at the women's domestic violence shelter in Orange. I began there because the Mary Kay charitable foundation brings awareness to domestic violence and research to women's cancers. I saw that we could make a difference right here in our own backyard. We get caught up with life and whatever life entails for each woman (kids, family, business, job, projects, church, working out). I started this journey six years ago to practice and do what makes my soul overjoyed, and that is to bring women a sense of empowerment through their inner beauty.

My strength and fortitude stems from my ultimate *Wonder Woman*, my mother. She taught me valuable practices, which help me to be a *Savvy Wonder Woman* in my own right! She was always my Wonder Woman, to me being as beautiful as Aphrodite and wise as Athena. She also always made sure we had time for some girl time. Even Wonder Woman would spend time with her mother and other Amazonian women for a spiritual recharge. It's a scientific fact that women who create regular genuine friendships and connect on a regular basis have stronger immune systems. Grab coffee, or get your pedis done together. You'll both benefit from the boost of energy from each other.

XIOMARA ESCOBAR is the CEO of *Xiomara Beauty* as an Independent Beauty Consultant with Mary Kay Cosmetics. She is a California native and has lived in South County for 25 years. She is a passionate, driven and compassionate woman who loves enriching women's lives by discovering the beauty of females from the inside out. Her belief is that confidence is the best makeup a woman can ever wear. She graduated from Chapman University with a BS in Marketing. She met her husband in college and has been married to him for 6 years with their baby, a 5 pound Maltese. She's been awarded Mary Kay's highest accolade Miss Go-Give; putting others first in her profession in 2012 in her unit.

XIOMARA'S *SAVVY WOMAN* TIPS

Posture – Stand tall with your legs apart and your hands on your waist. Increase assertive hormone testosterone and reduce stress hormone.

Beauty Sleep – Sleep reenergizes. Poor sleeping habits lower immune system and reduce the numbers of killer cells that fight germs.

Don't Take Everything so Seriously – Chronic stress causes decline in the system's ability to fight disease. Laughing activates stress-busting hormones and increases immune cells. Create a lifestyle of stress relieving activities like painting, Pilates or yoga.

Finding Solutions to the Problem – Assess situations and decisively act. Rely on your network of other heroines and join forces, or do it on your own to conquer the world or in other words, our obstacles.

Remember Where You Come From – Visit the homeland (parents) and let them know you love them.

Find out more about Xiomara at
www.TheDivaWearsPink.com

SURVIVOR

by Gillian Larson

My journey began in South Africa where I was born and raised, and then evolved when I met and married Ron, my wonderful American husband, 44 years ago. I was catapulted not only into my new life, but also into a country where the opportunities to do anything you want to do is in your hands.

I have always been adventurous and competitive and have many stories that have been woven into the threads of my life to make me the person I am now. It is not only my stories and experiences, but also the people who have been part of it all, and for that I am a very blessed woman. The most significant are my awesome family. I have always wanted to make a difference wherever I can to enhance others' lives, and my most recent experience has given me an enormous platform as a public figure to do so.

I believe that the success of my amazing life is due to my South African upbringing, which instilled in me drive, perseverance, creativity and my can-do attitude. My leadership skills come from the training ground we call "South African Schooling". Adopting the philosophy of Ubuntu at an early age, and my African soul, enhanced my spirit of caring and my need to make a difference in my world. The platform I was given was the American stage where YOU can do anything you want to do if you only believe in yourself and what you are capable of doing. This truly is the land of the free and I have taken it and run with it.

As frivolous as it may sound, I was chosen to be on the CBS TV show Survivor. After applying for eight years with a driving passion, I was picked when I was 61 years old. I am only one of two women over 60 to play. What I didn't realize was my driving passion to "get on Survivor" which I could never explain, was actually to be "off Survivor" and have that as a platform to spread the message of persistence, belief in oneself, and living life to the fullest, to make a difference where you can. I'm accomplishing this through motivational speaking, I've done over 410 engagements, and I will never tire of seeing how my talk impacts and helps others reach for their dreams and their capabilities. I collaborate with several charities, many are Military, lending my celebrity for their cause. I tell my story of persistence, dealing with disappointment, and never giving up. Be the best you can be. Everyone has a dream whether they are 2 or 102. My motto is *Dream it, Believe it, Prepare for it and Do it!*

I'm the proud creator and producer of Reality Rally, which is in its fifth year of production. In order to fully appreciate the amazing event Reality Rally has become, you must know the story. How did an event of this magnitude spring from the depth of disappointment? Why do over 100 Reality Stars from over 30 TV shows flock to Temecula every April? What draws over 600 volunteers to participate and make it what it is? Why do our amazing Sponsors help provide almost everything we eat, read, listen to, play and enjoy at prime venues throughout the town of Temecula, California? What encourages the Temecula organizations to be the Challenge Checkpoints in the Amazing Race type game?

Applying for Survivor for eight years, I was ready and prepared to play for 39 days and love every minute of it, but played for only six days. Little did I know as my Survivor flame was being snuffed out, the flame of Reality Rally was being ignited. Saddened and disappointed, I read a secreted message in my luxury item book from my daughter. "This is not over, something much greater is ahead of you." Sequestered in the jungle of Gabon, it struck a chord. What did it all mean? Perhaps the root of my passion to get on the show, and the reason for being booted off so soon, was in my hands. Reality Rally started forming. Celebrities, Charity, and City of Temecula became my *Fun for Funds* idea.

I knew the cause I wanted to support, with the same passion I had for Survivor (www.michellesplace.org). Michelle Watson died when she was 26 years old from breast cancer because she was told not to worry about a lump she found. I knew Reality Stars would like to have an opportunity to contribute in a positive and impactful way with their fame. I knew Temecula would embrace an event that would bring in money and exposure from all over the world, due to the Reality Star following. I formed my event tagline "Nobody makes a greater mistake, than he who did nothing because he could only do a little," Edmund Burke. This was the seed I knew would germinate and grow as Reality Rally. I knew that many would want to do their "little". I knew that people would come or support from afar; the ideal, the charity, the need, was the vehicle to do it.

That seed planted in my heart started with an idea, a budget of zero, and no funding. Due to a Production Team of 48, over 600 people, hundreds of Reality Stars and my supportive family, we all made it happen. Reality Rally has become a premier Reality Star event, it is one of Temecula's most attended events, bringing in money from over 16 countries and every one of the 50 States. It attracts people who want to do their "little" from all 50 States and approximately 512 cities around the world; to play, party, sponsor, donate and volunteer. Hundreds of Reality Stars from over 30 shows have raised funds and attended without compensation for our charity. Reality Rally is watched in over 96 countries and all over the USA due to the Reality Star component. What a crazy phenomenon Reality TV became, and I became part of it. How does one explain the involvement and excitement? All involved know why they get involved - passion, belief, and an honest interest in others. We are all volunteers, including myself, and I am in awe at how it all comes together.

This is a truly a weekend of *Fun for Funds*. We all have the *Fun,* and the clients of Michele's Place receive the *Funds.* I bow to all who have made my "jungle vision" such an awesome reality, and my amazing husband and family who support me all the way. We are going into our fifth year of production, and I will be forever grateful to all those who make it happen.

GILLIAN LARSON is a Reality Star from the TV show Survivor. She is competitive by nature and applied to Survivor 20 times in 8 years, never giving up and finally making it to Gabon. After, she developed Reality Rally, which is a trademarked fundraising business to raise funds with other Reality Stars. Gillian does motivational speaking engagements on *12 P's of Success and Dream Big*. She relates each of these principles to her Survivor experience, and is inspiring, powerful and entertaining. Gillian has been married for 44 years, has 3 married daughters and 7 grandchildren. Born and raised in Johannesburg, South Africa, she now devotes her time to making a difference in people's lives where she can.

GILLIAN'S *SAVVY WOMAN* TIPS

You Can Do Anything You Want to Do – Believe in yourself and what you are capable of doing.

Everyone has a Dream – My motto is *Dream it, Believe it, Prepare for it and Do it!*

Follow Your Dreams with a Driving Passion – The unbelievable can happen.

Contribute Your "Little" – It may affect more lives than you know.

"What counts in life is not the mere fact we have lived. It is the difference we have made to the lives of others that will determine the significance of the life we lead." ~ Nelson Mandela

Find out more about Gillian at
www.RealityRally.com
www.GillianLarson.com

HEALTH – BODY • MIND • SPIRIT

EMBRACE YOUR SOULFUL FREEDOM

by Mary Lou Hunter

I was living my life exactly the way I was supposed to. I was the perfect wife that cooked, cleaned, took care of my husband and daughter. I was the typical stay at home mom who lived a perfect life and told everyone that I had the best life. I was living my dreams. I really was the happiest I have ever been. I was the luckiest woman on earth because I had an awesome man to take care of me. I have a beautiful daughter to take care of. I had always known that my job was taking care of someone else. I did exactly what I was told, "Find a good man to take care of you."

Once my daughter started pre school I became bored and decided to go to college. This was a crazy concept for me because I was groomed to be a housewife and take care of my family. I had no clue that being a housewife was not what I wanted. I wanted to save the world and my husband approved as long as it did not interfere with my wife and mother duties. Little did I know that in order to do that, I had to become the authentic *me*. I started realizing how much I had masked my true feelings about myself, my life and my beliefs. I had no idea I was living in denial.

After four years of majoring in Psychology I started feeling depressed. My body ached to the point where I could not get out of bed. I had no energy and spent my days just laying around the house hiding from the world. This was hard for me because I was always on the go. To suddenly not having the energy to take my daughter to school was overwhelming and frightening.

When I went to the doctor, the first doctor told me that my pain was in my head and he told me I needed to seek therapy. The second doctor took my blood work and when the results came in, told me that I had Chronic Fatigue and said I would have to live a stress-free life and prescribed anti-depressant pills. Those pills made me sick and I felt like I was not even in my body. I seemed worse off than before, still did not have energy, and to top it off, I was spacey. After almost a decade, which I call my dark ages, I hit rock bottom.

I was physically sick and mentally unstable. I felt lost, lonely, depressed and confused. I was living at the opposite end of my dreams. I was the perfect example of a typical Pollyanna housewife, who on the outside seemed perfect, but on the inside was slowly dying. I was so angry that my life did not turn out the way I planned. I had been living my life as a lie, and no one knew my dark secrets of pain. How could I tell the world that I have everything that I thought I wanted and needed and yet, I was miserable? I kept asking myself, "How did I get here? Where did I go wrong? Why am I the only one in pain? I have an amazing life so what is wrong with me?"

At this point I knew I needed to drastically change my life. It was important for my health, and the health of my daughter. I realized the reason why I was sick was because I was my own roadblock. I was not authentic with my life, values and beliefs. I was only authentic with what I wanted to believe, what other people told me I should believe.

All my life I mostly valued acceptance. I needed to be the center of everyone's life. I needed to belong, and feel loved. I needed to be everyone's best friend, despite my true feelings. I never considered myself to be courageous, but I had to dig deep to find the courage to change so that I could heal.

When I realized that I was not taking care of me, I knew it was time to shift many things in my life. I had to become healthy again and feed my body the right nutrition. Change my values to match my current beliefs, change my rules so that I can be authentic with me, redefine my spiritual beliefs, and practice living in a higher vibration.

I began my healing process when I realized that I could be in control of my life. I was capable of making the right choices for my life. I was capable of living my life for me. The most fearful moment was when I let go of the idea of not being worthy. I was comfortable living a lie. I was extremely good at it.

There is a big difference in telling everyone you are happy when you are not, verses really *being* happy. All my barnacles were falling off and I started to feel alive for the first time in my life. I really had choices. I really had a voice. I was focusing on me for the first time in my life. Nourishing my mind, body and spirit made me feel whole for the first time in my life. I felt like a kid playing at a party, carefree, not looking back, nor forward, just living in the moment and soaking it all in. I WAS ALIVE. For the first time in my life I felt born again. I now call it *Organically-Born-Again*™; living my life authentic and in high vibration. Healing is more than just the physical. I needed to also look at my mental state and my spiritual beliefs. Once I put all the pieces together, my healing was complete.

Because of my own healing journey, I changed my career goals and started over again. I changed my focus to Holistic Health, and for the past 15 years I have been helping people find their freedom by focusing on Nutrition, Toxic Emotions and Spiritual Growth.

I never get tired of helping people embrace their Soulful Freedom. It's my mission to get people to their truth. It doesn't matter what your story is, the important things are: Where do you go from where you don't want to be? How do you free yourself from everything that holds you hostage? How do you get comfortable in your skin? How can you experience your Soulful Freedom?

MARY LOU HUNTER is a Shamanic Energy Healer, Counselor and Author of *Soulful Freedom*. She specializes in spiritual mind/body connections and has been helping her clients improve the quality of their lives for 20 years. Her expertise in bodywork with her knowledge of energy and nutrition offers a complete holistic experience. She has a Holistic Health Degree, and several certifications in nutrition, life coaching, aromatherapy, massage, hypnotherapy and Neuro-Linguistic Programming (NLP). Mary Lou is a Shamanic Reiki Master Teacher, a shamanic counselor, and an ordained Minister. She is finishing her doctorate in Holistic Life Coaching.

MARY LOU'S *SAVVY WOMAN* TIPS

Fuel Your Body with Proper Nutrition – Your body needs proper fuel so that you can thrive and have the energy to be successful.

Update Your Values According to Your Beliefs – It is important to understand why you value what you value, your motivation can be greater if you are in cause, and not effect.

Change Your Rules & Be Authentic to You – It's not in your best interest to live with rules that no longer serve your greater good. Change the rules that are not helping you meet your goals.

Be Congruent with Your Spiritual Beliefs – Our spiritual beliefs are very important to one's health. It is important to explore your beliefs so that you are personally invested in your spiritual empowerment.

Practice Living in a Higher Vibration – When you live in shame, fear, judgment and hate, you are living low vibration that is toxic and damaging to your success. Living in love, hope, acceptance, harmony and balance will assure you of success.

Find out more about Mary Lou at
www.MaryLouHunter.com

HEALTH – BODY · MIND · SPIRIT

WHAT'S YOUR VISION?

by Susie Augustin

Visual reminders are a powerful way to keep you focused on your goals. Three days after I created my vision board last month, my book *Sexy, Fit & Fab at Any Age!* was named Beverly Hills Book Awards Winner in the Beauty category. Wow! Last year it received the Body/Mind/Spirit award, which is a great testament to the message of the book, as well as becoming an Amazon Bestseller, #2 to Jessica Alba's new release! As a Beauty and Wellness Expert for over 15 years, and having won multiple awards as an author, speaker and publisher, this *Beauty* award is really important to me. I've worked as a branding expert and marketing copywriter with some of the world's most well-known and top rated beauty companies. To be recognized in the area of *Beauty* with this book that encourages women to embrace their uniqueness, in addition to their inner and outer beauty, makes me experience a new level of fabulous!

Just as exciting as it is for me to win accolades, it also brings me great pleasure when I lead others in creating their vision, coaching them in taking steps to achievement. To help entrepreneurs pursue their dreams and brand themselves through writing, I started Get Branded Press, providing book coaching, branding, copywriting, ghostwriting, editing, publishing and *Writing to Wow!* Workshops. My mission for Get Branded Press is *Dream it. Write it. Brand it.*

During the making of my latest book *Sexy, Fit & Fab Sirens* with 24 contributing authors, Claudia, one of the authors, shared with me her vision of an empowering book *Savvy Women Revving Up for Success.* She joined my *Writing to Wow!* Write Your Book in 6 Months Program, and we strategized on the message and structure of the book, including deciding on certain women to invite to be contributing authors. In the middle of developing the book, Claudia came to me with another project. She'd written a workbook *The 7 Mind Shifts,* to go with her coaching and mastermind groups, and asked me to help her with the editing and layout. I encouraged her to go one step further, as her content is incredible and should be available in book format to reach a broader audience. Exactly five months later *The 7 Mind Shifts* became an Amazon #1 Bestseller! As a bonus, I helped promote her first book, *From Dud to Stud: Revving Up for Success*, and it hit #2! Needless to say, we both experienced tears of happiness while on the phone with each other, celebrating her newest milestone over a glass of wine.

I wanted to toast Claudia in person, but I had recently relocated 100 miles away from friends and family for a career opportunity as a part-time branding expert for a good friend, while also focusing on Get Branded Press. Six months later my services were unexpectedly no longer needed, cutting my income in half, as well as losing my savings from investing everything to move, under the impression this was a long-term commitment. Needless to say, I felt disappointed, betrayed, regretted my decisions, alone and far from *home*.

I had a conversation with Claudia to discuss the book launch celebration I'd promised her and the other authors in my program (and *her* 20 contributing authors). I informed her there was no budget for the celebration or the book covers. But I had an obligation to my authors, so I would plan and keep moving forward. Through my tears I said that I was sure God would bless this situation and make it happen. I feel like I'm truly contributing, helping fabulous coaches and entrepreneurs get their stories out to help others and brand their businesses. Another one of my authors just hit #1 Bestseller on Amazon for her children's book.

Feeling a bit desperate and that I may need to give up *Writing to Wow!* Programs to get a full-time JOB, my friend Kim encouraged me follow my passion and dreams, continue to support my authors and expand my book coaching services. I started to journal and take long walks again (something I'd put aside since I moved, as I was "too busy working"). My mind started to expand and I dared to dream. I opened myself up by asking questions, "What do I really want? How am I able to make a contribution?" I tuned out the thoughts of being practical and doing the right thing, and what I thought people expected of me.

I got in tune with MY vision. It's amazing what happens when you visualize and focus. Remember when I mentioned that three days after I created my vision board I won a Beverly Hills Book Award in the Beauty category? Well, a section of my vision board represents PR for clients, and did I mention that Claudia's *The 7 Mind Shifts* was awarded

Winner in Leadership category and *From Dud to Stud* was Finalist in Personal Growth category? I was stunned by all the support we received when we posted our accomplishments on social media. Requests for my services came in from people wanting to write books and share their stories, asking for my all-inclusive *Writing to Wow!* Programs, ghostwriting, social media support and bestseller campaigns. Needless to say, I happily spent the weekend writing proposals for *Writing to Wow!* services. I decided I'll offer a one-year program, as well as monthly workshops, including my dream of having book writing beach retreats.

I feel happy and I feel hopeful. Going over the final edits and timeline for *Savvy Women Revving Up for Success,* I asked Claudia what she wanted me to write about (yes, even professional writers get writer's block!) Experiencing the unknown for the past several weeks as well as weight gain (doesn't chocolate, wine, and mac & cheese heal everything?), I felt compromised and vulnerable and didn't feel motivated to share one of my past successes when I am still figuring out the present. I realized that with my new ventures, I'd allowed my life to get way out of balance, neglecting my nutrition, exercise, friends, and spiritual time. When I realigned and focused on my vision and goals, creating a clear picture, everything around me started to change. Claudia said, "I want you to tell THIS story. You're already pulling yourself out of this, and you will inspire others to have the courage to do the same." She said I'm becoming the woman I'm meant to be.

My hopes are that YOU have a Vision, and take steps to make magic happen, fulfilling your dreams and the dreams of others around you!

SUSIE AUGUSTIN is the #1 Bestselling Author of *Sexy, Fit & Fab Sirens* and *Sexy, Fit & Fab at Any Age!* (and upcoming book *Writing to Wow!*) Her writing, publishing and speaking have garnered her several awards. She's a Beauty & Wellness Expert (a Licensed Aesthetician with a Marketing Degree) and worked as a branding expert and marketing copywriter with some of the world's top rated beauty companies. She started Get Branded Press to help others pursue their dreams and brand themselves through writing, offering *Writing to Wow!* Workshops. Susie inspires women of all ages to follow their passion, embrace their natural beauty and live a healthy lifestyle with her *Sexy, Fit & Fab*™ brand.

SUSIE'S *SAVVY WOMAN* TIPS

Have a Vision – Explore what makes you happy and uncover your talents. Sometimes it's hard to recognize the value of our gifts (what comes effortless to us) as we are taught that work should be "hard". What makes you feel excited?

Create a Vision Board – Visual reminders are powerful and keep you focused on your goals. When you have a choice to make and feel unsure, take a look at your vision board. What does it tell you?

Celebrate the Success of Others – I feel this is one of my secrets to success with Get Branded Press and *Writing to Wow!* Anyone who knows me knows that I have no qualms about promoting my brands, and I take just as much pleasure supporting others' dreams and brands.

Have the Courage to Dream – Go for it! Don't settle for mediocre, invest in yourself and enjoy the results.

Find out more about Susie at
www.GetBrandedPress.com
www.WritingtoWow.com
www.SusieAugustin.com
www.SexyFitFab.com

WEALTH

**Creating Wealth and Abundance
That Overflows to Contribution**

WEALTH

Money doesn't determine your wealth;
Real wealth is in the legacy you create for others.

The Bible states, "To whom much is given, much will be required." This is a beautiful reminder that if we have been entrusted with much: talents, wealth, knowledge, time, abilities and the like, it's required to give it back to benefit others. We find this cleverly paraphrased, in Uncle Ben's words of wisdom to Peter Parker in *Spiderman*, "With great power comes great responsibility."

It's from my own experience that I have found two truths, many more really, but for today... First, the more you have, the more opportunity you have to bless others. Second, you cannot outgive. The minute you give from your gifts and resources, it comes back even fuller and richer than before.

Over the past four decades, as I've lead thousands of individuals through the process of creating a Vision Board full of their dreams, I realize I've never seen a completed board that is only about financial wealth. It does appear, however, to be about creating *Happiness*. And happiness means something different to each of us. It might be dollars in the bank, security, being out of debt, and freedom to buy what we want. It could be building a life of comfort and being able to be with those you love. It may be having a healthy body and amazing relationships. It all falls in the area of Wealth and Abundance.

When I was a kid I loved to play outside, and one of my most favorite activities was lying on the lawn and peeking into my beautiful kaleidoscope. The colors were stunning, however, the speed of transformation was even more exciting. The colors changed quickly and were always creating new possibilities. Endless possibilities. I was always anxious to see what new color formation would show up; and this is how my life unfolded. Discovering what I could create and where that would take me.

Earlier, I shared with you the story of my Daddy and how his belief in me empowered me. Now I'd love to share with you how he taught me to put practical steps in place to have what I wanted in my life. It's more than a dream that moves you toward the outcomes you desire. Significant outcomes come from significant actions. Goals empower your dreams.

Remember, I was very young, probably around four and not in school yet. This was an amazing strategy and one that parents can use today to inspire their own children. Daddy would challenge me to earn money and make it fun. This is how he did it. We each had our own piggy bank. Mine was Mr. Peanut (I saved Planter Peanut wrappers to earn this) and his was just a plain canning jar. The challenge was to see who could fill their bank with the most coins by the date set on the calendar. It's always important to put a date for your goals. The winner got to capture the piggy bank of the other. Wow, what high stakes. Believe me I wanted to win, and Daddy would cleverly let me count his bank every day if I wanted, to determine who was ahead. Of course, we know he had perfect control over this game, but I didn't. I worked really hard to earn money, and to not spend any more money than needed which allowed me to have more coins than he had saved. He would inch ahead of me, and motivated me to go find ways to make more money.

"Small opportunities are often the beginning of great enterprises."
~ Demostheses

At this point I started my first business, selling walnuts. I started by taking orders first. Then doing the work of picking up the walnuts and stuffing them into my gunny sack that trailed behind me. Bringing the walnuts home, decorating brown lunch sacks with my gorgeous drawings and flowers from Mother's garden, then packaging and delivering my product - walnuts. I still remember to this day just how it felt when the coins were placed in my hand for the delivery, along with the smile of the customer. Eagerly, I'd rush home and add the coins to my piggy bank. What a sense of satisfaction. Yes, there were times I won and times I lost. But I became good at figuring out how to win.

I didn't spend my winnings. I quickly learned how to roll coins, even before I could read or knew any math. I would proudly carry my "bank deposit" with me when I went to the bank with Mom. Standing on my tiptoes to reach the counter, I'd push my sack of rolled coins and my little savings passbook to the teller and watch with an anxious heart to get my savings passbook back. I'd look at the numbers growing and my heart would race. Still today, I love figuring out ways to make money and save it, but the next thing I needed to learn back then was how to *share* it.

It wasn't long before my folks found ways for me to help others, and even though I was reluctant at first, it became fun to find ways to share. I can tell you that it truly is more blessed to give than receive, and this philosophy has been a huge part of my journey.

Even though I still love making money today, I love helping others do the same thing. But the real beauty is seeing the joy someone has when they have blessed the life of another, either through sharing their gifts, resources, knowledge, abilities and/or financially, and to know they are making a difference in the world today.

The last thought I must share is to have fun. Whether it is traveling, singing, dancing, painting, or playing with your kids or grandkids. Plan fun into every day, every week, every month and every year. Laugh as much as possible. Enjoy every moment. Celebrate.

PLAYING MY BEST GAME, AND HOW TO PLAY YOURS

by Patti Cotton

As the oldest of four girls, growing up felt like being one of many puppies in a box! We were blessed with wonderful parents who raised us with lots of love and care. It was challenging to parcel out individual attention and praise in such a lively group, and as the oldest, I learned to command some of this when I accomplished or achieved something noteworthy. Was my spelling paper perfect, my room spotless? If so, I was told how "good" I was. Was there a comma or a pillow out of place? This was also quickly pointed out for correction, and I would scramble to fix it. Producing and "being perfect" were great ways to fill the hunger for attention. But it also unwittingly sent the message that what I *did* was valuable – not who I *was*. With this priming, you can guess that as the years advanced, I continued to look for validation through "doing" and "being perfect" (as if one can ever reach that perfection). The classroom was my favored playground for recognition, and overachievement was part of what made me feel like "enough."

Later, as a young mother, I continued to seek validation in a very difficult marriage. I found myself as chief and only breadwinner for the family. It became evident that this situation would not change, and so I worked one job at first, and then two, to ensure that my children had what they needed. During this time, I also attended school so that I could get ahead and care better for the family.

Of course, I am of the belief that we need to do what we can before turning to others for help, and so I feel that this course of action was right. Admittedly, however, I felt pride and worth when I received praise from my extended family for the self-sacrifice I was making. The praise was certainly given in the spirit of encouragement, but the faulty message was in keeping with what I had learned: I am worthy by the amount of what I achieve and accomplish.

Promotions came easily and consistently over the following years, until one day, I found myself in charge of fundraising for five hospitals, making a healthy six-figure income. Leading a team of 15 wonderful professionals, I continued to seek affirmation of my self-worth through achieving impossible goals others set in front of me. If they said something couldn't be done, I'd figure out how to do it. If someone mentioned that no one could figure out a problem, I would find the answer.

Ultimately, this deadly approach to life found our fundraising team raising amazing sums of money in situations where others had not accomplished the numbers. However, the vicious drive to overachieve found me near burnout. Something had to change. It was clear that no matter how much I achieved, it would never be enough. How could I break this deadly trap, and yet recognize the worth I brought to the world? Who was I, without achieving the impossible goals of others? Would I be loved and appreciated just for being myself? This began a soul-searching process that would ultimately prompt me to turn from a prestigious corporate career, and to respond to my true calling – that of awakening the potential of others and their self-worth.

This soul-searching process began with the question, "What is self-worth?" And the answer, upon careful reflection, was that it is not what you do, or how much you achieve, but who you are as a child of God with the natural gifts you bring to the world. As I set out to find my own natural gifts, I was hungry for learning about human development, so I chose to return to school for a degree in organizational management and development, with a dedicated focus in coaching. This life choice led me to find myself - the value of me - and ultimately, my calling.

Coaching is a process which requires you to discover, rediscover, reclaim, and celebrate who you are as you learn to help others do the same. It is a way to get in touch to see what you want to do with this information, where you want to be, and what you would like to do with your gifts to make a difference in the world. One of the beautiful things about the process is that you give yourself permission to be who you are and live your life as you desire, leaving behind the expectations of others. Your goals, your dreams, your vision – they are all yours.

In returning to student mode, I discovered personal gifts of compassion, intuition, and guidance. This inspired me to vision a coaching business of my own, through which I could facilitate others celebrating their personal gifts and how they wanted to contribute to the world.

Since my own awakening, I have coached hundreds of individual clients and groups to reclaim their own gifts and direction, and to reach the goals of their choosing. I have coached leaders, executives, and other chief decision-makers and their teams around the world who are ready to step into more of their potential. I have also coached silenced and vulnerable voices that have made the courageous decision to move beyond barely surviving to thriving.

Each of us is created with unlimited potential and an ability to impact the world in a way that no one else can. With the right help and support, we can tap into our unique gifts, learn how to use them, and step into so much more of what we were created to be. Life's experiences can get in the way and keep us playing small. What excites and motivates me is to help others break through to play their best and biggest game, so that they can make the change in the world they were meant to make.

PATTI COTTON is PCC-Certified with the International Coach Federation and a certified mediator for the State of California. She holds advanced certifications to help facilitate change and resolve conflict. Patti's advocacy supports alternatives for domestic violence and the empowerment of vulnerable and silenced voices. She has over 25 years of international leadership experience and has worked alongside heads of state around the globe. She is known for breaking through impossible barriers to produce exceptional results, and helps executives and teams accomplish their visions and goals. Patti has Master's Degrees in Organizational Management & Development and in English Literature.

PATTI'S *SAVVY WOMAN* TIPS

Know Your Unique Gifts – Comparing yourself to others will find you coming up short every time. Be you – no one else can do it!

Make a Difference with Your Gifts Daily – Gifts and talents are meant to be shared, to impact the world in a positive way. Use yours, and use them always.

Know Your Core Values and Live by Them – List your top 5 values and keep them with you to help make decisions and take actions.

Confront Tough Issues – Avoiding confronting your issues will rob you of energy, focus, and confidence. Confront it, get over it, move forward.

Be Courageous – Where are you playing it small? How is playing it small in this area cheating the world? Be honest, be daring, and be ruthless to ferret out any fear-based mindsets or behaviors that keep you from making your contributions in the world.

Find out more about Patti at
www.PattiCotton.com

HOW DID I GET HERE?

by Kelli C. Holmes

I found myself asking that question many times during the hardest three years of my life. That season of life taught me a lot of things, but the one that sticks with me most is that it's not what you've been through in life that defines you; it's how you get through it!

Ever been in one of those situations in life that is really rough? You know the kind of struggle that shakes you to your very core? And yet, as hard as that challenge is, it somehow becomes a bold and defining moment for you. How are you going to handle it? How are you going to make it through? You know, it's the "how" that means the most.

People can throw anything at you and you CAN be better for it. I truly believe that today. Not long after starting my business, I was served with a multimillion-dollar lawsuit by the biggest competitor in my industry. A lawsuit with the absolute best lawyers one could buy and the best mud they could sling at me, and all at a time of great challenge to me. I had just turned 40, felt like I was starting over again, had two kids under the age of 3, and a brand new business; you know, just a few things to keep me a little stressed out! But isn't that the way it always is? Cars break down on the way to a big meeting, contracts and business transactions get cancelled at the seemingly worst possible time, life just happens sometimes like that. I say, "So what?" Hear me when I say whatever struggle you face, you can make it to the other side. It's not *what* you've been through in life that defines you; it's *how* you get through it!

It's the HOW that I want you to care about. You may not win all of your battles, but that isn't the important part. How you get to the other side of the struggles you are faced with is very telling, though. It is telling of your character, your belief system, how you approach life, and how you view the future. Your struggles, your setbacks, or your past (and trust me on this one, because I have a doozy of a past), do not define you. It is the way you handle these struggles, setbacks, and past decisions that mean the most. That was key for me in my three year legal battle (war). I knew that I had done the right thing and I was not about to let a bully tell the courts, the world, or me, otherwise.

How did I get through my David vs. Goliath battle? I had faith. Faith in God; faith in myself. I also had a great deal of support from those around me: my family (a husband who was pulling double duty supporting us financially and extra childcare while I was off playing lawyer to protect my company); my friends (one friend who was with me throughout one entire trial, taking notes for me, praying with me, propping me up when all I wanted to do was give up); and my team (my staff at TEAM Referral Network); and my faith, did I mention faith? I also had the balls (can I say balls after I have talked about God?) and determination that this lawsuit was NOT going to shut me down, no way, no how. That meant 4:00 am mornings getting work done before my babies woke up. That meant refinancing the house to figure out other ways to keep my business afloat. That meant countless tears from exhaustion mixed with stress and anger. That meant learning as much as I could to represent myself in this intense legal battle. All the while, remaining true to the core belief that what I was doing was the right thing. Remember the question I started with? "How did I get here?" was never far from my mind.

Once that legal battle was done, and we were victorious on all counts, I rejoiced. I really felt like I wanted to take the longest nap in history, but I rejoiced nonetheless. The dust settled after that sweet sound of the federal court judge dismissing the case and ending that three year fight. I was free to grow, but I wasn't the same me anymore. This had changed me. Nothing scared me anymore. My concept of what I considered threatening had shifted entirely. My map of "fear" looked completely different and I was free. My convictions had been right and I had won. Perseverance with a dose of tenacity had developed boldness in me like no other. In retrospect, I can see it as a gift.

After the initial celebrating was done, we decided to celebrate everyday by rocking it with TEAM Referral Network. The success of overcoming a legal onslaught simply meant that it was time to get back to the business of life and my company. It's amazing what you can accomplish when you can put your focus on growth! The year following the end of all the legal proceedings enabled me to grow the company by 56%! In that same year, we also hit the five year magic milestone in business. We were real and here to stay!

There may be people out there who want to crush your spirit and keep you from succeeding. They may want to stop you and your business from thriving. Maybe… your biggest foe is you! Don't let them (or yourself) crush you. Don't let that little voice inside tell you that you can't get to the other side of your struggle victoriously, with integrity and remain true to who you are.

As business owners, and especially as women in business, we need to go *all in*. The world needs more female CEOs, franchisors, business owners/entrepreneurs. Women have a unique perspective and personality to bring to the table. We can, and we *should* do it! The world needs more women who are ready to bring their passion, acumen and integrity in business to change the world.

I've always been passionate about helping entrepreneurs succeed, which is a huge part of why TEAM Referral Network was created. My legal struggle early on simply gave me more drive to help even more entrepreneurs. But, I don't want them to simply succeed; I want them to thrive. My thoughts are if you're going to go do this, you may as well go BIG! Don't let yourself get sidetracked by the inevitable obstacles that will come your way. You can do this! You will do this! And, I can't wait to see it when you do!

KELLI C. HOLMES is the CEO/Founder of the revolutionary networking organization TEAM Referral Network and its sister company TEAM Franchise Corp. TEAM has opened hundreds of chapters, with thousands of members throughout the U.S. and is launching TEAM Australia and Taiwan later this year! She is the Author of *Effective Networking - Is Your Networking NOT Working?* and her upcoming book *God...How the Hell Did I Get Here?* She's an expert in teaching entrepreneurs how to grow their business in big ways. Kelli is a child of God, wife, Mom, CEO, Speaker, Radio/Webcast guest, CEO Space Faculty Member and travels the country teaching on networking and relationship marketing.

KELLI'S *SAVVY WOMAN* TIPS

Have FAITH – Believe in God, believe in yourself.

Go BIG – Going 10 times bigger is the same, and sometimes even easier, as going just a little big, and it's more fun!

Stick to It – Stickability is one of the single most important qualities to becoming successful. Most people quit when things get tough. Be a part of the few who persevere.

Surround Yourself with a Good TEAM – You cannot do it all by yourself. Surround yourself with the right team and you will have the support system to go ROCK it everyday.

Give Back – Find a cause near and dear to you, and incorporate it into your life, your work, and even your company. My company has our TEAM "Community Outreach" program, and we work with many awesome non-profits, raising tens of thousands of dollars and hundreds of friends for them.

Find out more about Kelli at
www.TeamReferralNetwork.com

WEALTH – CREATE A LEGACY

BE THE BLESSING FOR SOMEONE ELSE

by Linda Van Kessler

Most 8-year-olds don't dream of working in The White House, but that's exactly what I was determined to do. At age 19, I achieved that dream by becoming a Staff Assistant to President Ford at The White House. Following his term in office, I moved to Palm Springs, CA with him and became Director of Scheduling and Press for President and Mrs. Ford. I went on to become Director of Scheduling and Press for Dr. Robert Schuller at the Crystal Cathedral in Garden Grove, CA. After, I spent 28 years working in crusades around the world with Dr. Billy Graham. I then opened my own public relations, booking and management company in Beverly Hills, CA representing some of the world's greatest talent and authors. I married a doctor, traveled the world, had an incredible son and in short – was living the dream!

And then the phone call came. My husband had gone to work, suffered a massive heart attack and died at his desk. Stunned and dazed, my biggest focus became how to get out of bed each day to take care of my 15-year-old son. I was widowed at age 49, and a few years later my only son left home for college. I was left with sadness, a bad case of empty nest syndrome and a longing for the way things used to be, feeling that my greatest moments in life were over. I had spent my life caring for my family but felt unfulfilled that I had truly made a difference in the world. My dream had always been to work with children in some capacity, as that is my true love.

An incredible man, Charles, came into my life. He shared the same love for children that I did. In fact, he had started a children's charity because, at age two, he himself had seen his family snatched away in front of him by the Nazis during World War II in Amsterdam, Holland. He was placed in a state run orphanage enduring abuse of every kind and surviving on flower bulbs. We married and were determined that we were going to make a difference in the world.

Our charity is Passion 4 K.I.D.S. I was looking for a child to help when God suddenly "interrupted" my life as I picked up the newspaper to read about a baby being wheeled in his stroller on the sidewalk by his grandpa on the way to the park. They were violently hit by a teen driver, drunk and high, leaving the baby blind, paralyzed and in a coma. I went to the hospital to find that child, and from that moment on we have been consumed with every possible way to help that young family. We spent one year raising $100,000 to put a down payment on a small home for the family, which had to be renovated to become handicapped accessible. We arranged for 64 San Diego based businesses to do an extreme home makeover and donate the labor and supplies. Our charity has become almost a full-time job that leaves me no time for self-pity or pessimism, but instead floods me with overwhelming joy for the life I have been blessed with. Passion 4 K.I.D.S. is now gaining national recognition and busier than ever.

It is not easy to be optimistic when you focus on yourself, your circumstances and your problems (I'm getting old, life is passing me by, my kids don't need me anymore, etc.) But I have found that turning your focus to helping others is the key to becoming optimistic, and making the next chapter of your life have purpose and meaning. You don't have to look far to find someone who is in a lot more pain than you are. Getting involved in the life of a hurting person brings you much more blessing even than the person you are helping, and in turn your gratitude for your life grows exponentially. I look outward instead of inward for meaning. I spend time with our kids in our charity that so desperately need attention, love, and just someone to care. I give out all the hugs, kisses, love and efforts to make their young lives better that I possibly can. I come back to my reality refreshed, renewed and refilled totally with the love they reciprocate to me. That's why love is a circle.

We have been interviewed by media around the country about our charity and story, something I never thought would ever happen. San Diego declared April 15 "Passion 4 K.I.D.S. Day". The California State Assembly honored our charity. We were featured on the front page of the San Diego Union Tribune as people making a difference in San Diego. I say this not for self-aggrandizement, but rather to marvel at the way God can take a seemingly tragic situation and turn it into something that can make a difference for so many people hurting. When you let God "interrupt" your life, amazing things happen even in the midst of overwhelming hardship and sorrow.

I hope Charles and I can be an example of two very ordinary people – no prior experience in setting up a non-profit, middle class with few resources, helping with situations we previously knew nothing about – who stepped out of our comfort zone to let God "interrupt" our life with a purpose and mission we are passionate about, yet totally inadequate in our own strength to accomplish. We have learned over and over when God gives the vision, He gives the provision.

We hope you will be inspired to ask yourself, "If not me, who? If not now, when?" Find your passion, step out in faith and start! We're sure you'll find, like us, that the blessing you receive is far greater than the blessing you can be.

LINDA VAN KESSLER is the CEO of Passion 4 Life liquid vitamins and minerals and Co-Founder with her husband of Passion 4 K.I.D.S. non-profit charity. She worked at The White House for President and Mrs. Ford, with Dr. Billy Graham in his crusades around the world, and with Dr. Robert Schuller at the Crystal Cathedral. She makes her home in San Diego, CA with her husband and soul mate, Charles. She is the proud mom of a wonderful son, Rali, and blessed with a "daughter-in-love" (rather than daughter-in-law) Mary. Every spare moment finds Linda with her three precious grand-angels - Cici, Jason and Henley.

LINDA'S *SAVVY WOMAN* TIPS

G – **Give** a voice to your dream.

I – **Intentionally** meet people who can help you.

V – **Visualize** the end result.

E – **Expect** and embrace obstacles.

R – **Remember** it's ALWAYS about others.

Find out more about Linda at
www.Passion4LifeVitamins.com
www.Passion4Kids.org

ACHIEVE THE IMPOSSIBLE

by Laura Neubauer

It's interesting how just one challenge, well one pretty big challenge, can deliver so many lessons to help prepare us to handle future obstacles. When I began my company I had no money, no plan, and a big million dollar loan. Some thought I had it easier than others. You see, my company wasn't a startup, I had acquired it. So, unlike startups where your expenses increase with the growth of your company, my expenses were already well established.

After being in business for 30 days, I didn't have a financial plan in place. I never really thought about how to pay my employees *before* my receivables were collected. When it came time to process my first payroll, the total was $40,000. After calculating the payroll amount, I went to my online banking, but discovered that I had only $4,000 in the business account. I went to my PO Box, thinking maybe I received money, but it was not the case. I went to the bank asking for assistance, but being a new business account at the bank, they couldn't help me.

So I went home and I cried and cried. And just when I thought I couldn't cry anymore, I did, and I cried a lot. The thoughts kept going through my head, "I am not going to make payroll on Monday. My workforce is going to stop working. My company is going to crash in its first 30 days in business. And I'll still have that million dollar loan. So I got up and started thinking about solutions for how to fix this. It was Friday afternoon and I called everyone I could call, asking for help; my friends and family, my business acquaintances, and even a few of my enemies. I was in trouble and I desperately needed help. I even called that little stack of business cards on my desk. You know the ones. The ones of the people you just met that week. Now there were plenty of great ideas offered, but no one had the solution to my problem.

So later that afternoon, I went back to the bank and withdrew all the money in the account. Then I hit the road and went to Las Vegas. Yes, I was going to bankroll my cash to make sure we made payroll on

Monday. I felt power inside me, filled with inspiration and desperation, walking the casino floor with an attitude. I would take down the house.

Well, I didn't make $40,000 that weekend, but I did increase my cash on hand. Anyhow, I had to come back home and be a big girl and take care of my problem. Upon my return there was a message on my answering machine. Someone was willing to help me make payroll. We worked out the terms of the agreement, and then I was instructed not to worry, that I would have the money in my account by three o'clock Monday afternoon. That began the very first policy ever written at my company. *You do not get your paycheck until 3:00 in the afternoon.*

I do not suggest my wild solution to everyone, but I learned important lessons. Lessons that have prepared me to overcome other challenges in life. Being prepared is the key. The quicker we push through the challenges, we can better prepare ourselves to see opportunity. Success really begins when you can see the opportunities in front of you, and sometimes you are even able to create your own. Opportunities are always there, but if you are stuck in your obstacles, you may miss them.

As business women, we think we need to be strong, so we fail to ask for help. We have our "sales face" on all the time and act like everything is perfect. We struggle when it comes to asking for help. Why are we afraid? Rejection? How is someone is going to see me if I ask them for help? Will I be perceived as weak? No! Let's look at this a bit differently. It is not about what others will think about you. It is about how others feel when asked. How would you feel if someone asked you for help? You would be honored. Your view of the relationship would be elevated. You are now considered to be close and special, someone respects you so much that they have asked *you* for help. And if you could help them, wow, that's even better. There are people who would love and would be honored to help you!

During the time of challenges, we live with so much stress. We kill ourselves with the stress and burden of worry. The feeling is horrible. You know that feeling. It's nasty, it's bad and it's unproductive. Let me share with you a thought, "Worry is a feeling about an event that hasn't even happened yet. And most of the time that event never happens." That's right, most of the time it never happens. Yet we let it eat us up. Stop it! Stop worrying.

Sometimes we don't move forward because we are not ready. Lacking confidence can paralyze our movement. Keep moving! Do not handicap yourself because you're not ready, you'll figure it out. And here's a secret. We are never ready. Plus, you do not have to do it all. Creating your professional dream team will give you the additional support you need; whether that is your professional team, CPA, lawyers etc., or an advisory board for you to bounce ideas off of. I must say I think I increase my IQ just by hanging out with some pretty wicked smart people.

I play a big game! We work too hard to be average. So if you're going to play - *play BIG!* I'll be honest, I think I play as big as I can so that I have room for error, because believe me, I make plenty of mistakes. Plus, why should we be satisfied with where we are? Play for another purpose, bigger than yourself, and you'll find that it's easier to play a bigger game. I measure my success in job creation, and every time I add to my staff, I am very grateful that the bigger I get, the more I can do.

Finally, find your inner bad ass! Get into your zone. When I walked across that casino floor I felt like I could do anything. And I can do anything! Being mentally prepared creates the strength within us to achieve, what we may think at the time, the impossible. Having a strong state of mind will give you the confidence, personal inspiration, energy and power to achieve your success.

LAURA NEUBAUER is a Professional Bad Ass and the founder of Deliver It, an overnight, same day and customized delivery company. Her exceptional business acumen coupled with her grit and entrepreneurial spirit grew Deliver It into a multi-million dollar company in just a few years. Laura has been recognized as Orange County's *Entrepreneur to Watch,* and in 2011 she was honored as California's *Business Woman Of The Year.* In 2012, Deliver It was recognized as one of Inc's fastest growing companies in America. Laura's success is based on integrity, creative solutions and out of the box business concepts, strong relationships, and the passion to see other people succeed.

LAURA'S *SAVVY WOMAN* TIPS

Ask for Help – Don't be afraid to ask for help. There are people who would love and would be honored to help you!

Stop Worrying – Worry is a feeling about an event that hasn't even happened yet. And most of the time that event never happens.

Build a Dream Team – Get help and give help with your professional connections.

Play Big – Be daring, don't be average or mediocre. Have the confidence to play full out.

Get in Your Zone – Being mentally prepared creates strength and confidence. Achieve the impossible.

Find out more about Laura at
www.BadAssBiz.biz
www.Deliver-It.com

MILLION DOLLAR PhD
FROM THE SCHOOL OF HARD KNOCKS

by Stacey O'Byrne

When it came to money, I had a belief that I was really good at making it. I also thought that I perfected the art of losing it. I did exactly what I was told to do growing up. I got great grades in school, I went to a good college, and got a great education. I even joined the US Army to serve my country and help build a more solid independent foundation for myself. After I was honorably discharged from my military service, I invested the next 12 years of my life in growing my corporate career. I had successfully climbed the corporate later and made a very comfortable six-figure income.

After the tragic events of September 11, 2001, I found myself painfully unemployed. I was devastated, and truth be told, felt disposable. As many out there, I found myself unable to find a job that could support my family. I found myself really scared and doubtful for the first time in my life; however I had a comfortable financial cushion, so I knew I would be ok for an extended period of time.

After several months of tirelessly seeking employment, I had made the decision that I would create a job for myself. This is where my journey as a business owner and an entrepreneur began. This is also where I earned my *Million Dollar PhD*, from the school of hard knocks. I was introduced to a man who owned a failing company. He approached me to be a business partner so I could help him turn the company around. We did just that. We built a thriving seven-figure business in a very short period of time.

A series of unexpected challenges changed the course of my career. I crushed my hand with a three hundred pound box and needed seven surgeries to rebuild it. In addition, things between my business partner did not work out. If you have ever had a business partner, what I am about to share with you may not surprise you. Not only did they not work out, but they ended very ugly. I was left with sixteen cents in the bank, a very ugly lawsuit between the both of us; which lasted for over four years. Did I mention he sued me? I was going to walk away and request mediation. I really just wanted my half, what was right. But he had to fabricate a lawsuit so he could manipulate the system to get more. I quickly went from a near perfect FICA to having to make one of the most difficult decisions of my life and that was file bankruptcy and walk away from everything I worked so hard to build, the seven figure business, the million dollar commercial building we bought, pretty much in short, almost everything.

This all quickly started a downward spiral for me. For the first time ever in my life, I had no money. I was broke. At a time when unemployment was at its highest and our economy was at its worst. I was focusing on everything I didn't want, buying into my story, walking around as a victim and forgetting all the tools I had spent years learning. I was allowing my net-worth dictate my self-worth. I was so stuck in my story I wasn't able to move forward.

I didn't allow myself to stay stuck long. I couldn't, I had a family depending on me, a daughter looking up to me. I had always had the belief and understanding that what we feed grows, and what we starve dies. We hear time and time again to focus on what we want, as opposed to what we don't want. I made the decision. Yes, I said the decision, to switch from a disempowering mindset to a more empowering mindset, or as I like to refer to it, a success mindset. I may have fallen down, or some may view it, as I had been kicked down, but reality for me is that I really had a choice. I could stay down, stay disempowered and feel like a victim, which I may have had every right to feel. Or, I could pick myself up, ask myself different questions that would create a more focused empowering state and forge forward and shift my reality. We all have the same choices continually in our lives as problems, or as I like to refer to them as *learnings*, present themselves in our lives. You see, I believe that choice is a powerful thing and that suffering is always optional. I tell myself this any time I am faced with a situation, a *learning*. This belief, this understanding helps me move out of situations quickly, or better yet rarely experience them now at all. This belief, this mindset helps me stay empowered, live a successful life, have successful businesses and relationships and live life as I believe I am supposed to, and that is by continually designing my destiny.

I have built The Success Mastery Academy and created Success Mastery Systems. These help people develop viable tools and skills to create the life they deserve, design the destiny that they have always dreamed and desired. I have worked with thousands of people both personally and professionally, and have watched them transform their lives and their businesses and walk fully in their deserved empowered. I live the most rewarding life watching people transform their lives and live their dreams. I live my passion and I live my purpose and I am grateful every day for every *learning* that came my way because I know now that without those *learnings*, without those gifts, I would not be where I am today. I have learned to embrace the adversity that could have held me down because I know deep in my heart that it was really presented in my life to build me up and make me who I am today, so I would have the knowledge and tools to help so many others stand in and embrace their empowerment and live the life they have always wanted.

I'm grateful to be able to share my *learnings* with you; which you could chose to implement in your life, put in your tool belt. There are no answers in a *why?* *question*, there is only the story, and the story doesn't serve moving you forward. Change your questions to more empowering questions that can create movement. They start with: how? what? when? where? Never *why?*

STACEY O'BYRNE is a Speaker, Trainer, Bestselling Author, Success Coach, Certified NLP Master Trainer, US Army Veteran, and TEAM Referral Network Franchise Owner. She has over 20 years experience as a successful sales professional, manager, leader, business owner and entrepreneur. Stacey has built one 7-figure business and two 6-figure businesses by practicing what she preaches. She helps entrepreneurs, small business owners, and salespeople realize their dreams and make them a reality. She understands challenges that today's professionals experience, the value in personal and professional development, how it influences one's performance as a salesperson and business owner.

STACEY'S *SAVVY WOMAN* TIPS

Tool Belt – Implement smart practices into your daily life.

Choice is Powerful – Suffering is always optional.

Bad Situations in Life Don't Break You – They make you.

Changing Your Current Reality – As easy as changing your mind.

Always, Always, Always Develop Yourself – What you feed grows and what you starve dies.

Find Yourself Stuck? – Ask yourself different questions.

Find out more about Stacey at
www.PivotPointAdvantage.com

DIVINE GUIDANCE

by Linda L. Smith

In 1992, I became the President and Founder of Four-D College, a fully accredited vocational school providing high quality career training at campuses in Colton, CA and Victorville, CA. I am also the proud published author of *Business by Faith*, a trilogy of books that highlight my incredible journey of faith from disheartened child to influential college president. My unique journey also serves as the basis for many of my motivational talks. As a highly sought after speaker, I am honored to empower and educate a variety of audiences from youth and teens to entrepreneurs and seasoned professionals.

With Christian values and beliefs, Four-D College's experienced instructors prepare students to work with patients and communities to address health issues, prevent illness, and maintain the best physical, emotional, and spiritual health treatment plans. We provide classroom lecture learning, clinical rotation experience, and mold students to become ethical healthcare professionals of integrity. To date, Four-D College is proud to have more than 7,000 graduates who have launched rewarding, fulfilling careers.

Running a business poses many financial challenges. Having the responsibility to the business to cover expenses such as payroll, various insurances, supplies, equipment, and marketing is overwhelming at times.

There have been many times when the monthly cash flow did not cover the monthly expenses. I had to pray and be still so I could have a clear head. I needed to focus on the direction that God would give. Where I took the necessary steps to address the cash shortage, I know it was divine inspiration.

I contacted the bank and spoke with the branch manager. I explained the financial situation and asked that the bank cover the payroll and all checks. I had to pay out of my own pocket until I received expected deposits. He agreed to cover all checks for a week. He approved a verbal loan for thousands of dollars. That was years ago. Divine guidance and the bank manager's unprecedented actions kept me in business.

I am always grateful I have my personal relationship with God. I know that the success of my business is not due to being an outstanding business woman. I believe the success of my business and the longevity of Four-D College is due to my obedience to the will of God and the call to serve in my life. I celebrate by giving thanks for God's grace. The celebration is not a look at how great I have done. My celebration is at how great God is.

In turn, I have helped others facing obstacles. I have always extended a hand of kindness to others to help them through tough personal and financial challenges. I have paid medical bills; I have paid a student's rent for seven months; I have paid balances for a wedding dress: and I covered the closing cost to help a young couple obtain a home. I believe God always replenishes the unselfish acts of a kind heart.

I am inspired to see the potential in a person and guide them to levels beyond their imagination. I encourage my staff and guide them to perform their responsibility to a higher level so they may achieve increased personal growth. My philosophy is if a person has an idea to improve a process, a procedure, or a department, then it becomes their responsibility to move forward with the idea and bring it to fruition. Whether it is an idea to make a change to a curriculum, changes to a program, or suggestions for better departmental operations, it is those ideas developed that bring expanded growth. Those who are motivated to learn more and take on more responsibility should be given the opportunity to demonstrate their capabilities. I get excited when I watch the accomplishments of my teammates.

LINDA L. SMITH, MBA, BSN, RN is founder and president of Four-D College and is the Author of *Business by Faith,* a Contributing Author of *Creating Value through People,* and has been featured in Essence Magazine. In October 2013 a documentary, *A Profile In Courage, Linda L. Smith* was released. She was appointed Board of Trustees for the Loma Linda Ronald McDonald House and to the California State Assistance Fund for Enterprise, Business and Industrial Development Corporation Board of Directors by Governor Brown's Office.

LINDA'S *SAVVY WOMAN* TIPS

Collaboration – Know that one's success is the result of others who have worked with you.

Remain Humble and Keep Your Feet on the Ground – It is fine to acknowledge your success, but never boast or brag.

Never be Afraid to Ask for Help – There are many individuals who are smarter, more politically astute, and more financially stable than one may have in-house. A network of colleagues to call upon is invaluable.

Have a CPA/Accountant That You Can Trust – Always know where your money is. Keep an honest person honest by not giving them total access to your funds. Either myself or my Vice President (husband) sign all checks in our company.

Connect with Your Community and Give Back

Find out more about Linda at
www.LindaLSmith.com

RELATIONSHIPS

**Building Strong Relationships
With Yourself and Others**

RELATIONSHIPS

Treat your relationships like a garden.
Plant the best of seeds; water, feed and nurture.
Then you will harvest riches beyond your highest hopes.

Each morning when I arrive in my kitchen, I stare out my window to our water fountain where I watch one hummingbird show up regularly. Once the first one shows up, others start to appear. As very energetic birds, you would think they might be too busy to have friends and to cultivate friendships. However, they totally enjoy being connected with others. They dart around playfully for a bit, then off they go to take care of the responsibilities of their day. Nature shows us the beauty in friendships.

People often ask me about my long marriage, fifty years plus. Just recently a young woman asked me how we created such a long-lasting relationship. She really wanted some specifics, so I shared the essence of building any quality relationship, as I believe to be true. These are the key ingredients: Love, Trust, Forgiveness, Celebrating our likenesses and differences, Respect, and always practicing great Communication (listening more than talking). She smiled and seemed grateful. I might not ever see her again, however, my hope is that she'll practice these simple ingredients to building a beautiful life.

I believe relationships have a divine order. The first and most important relationship for me is my spiritual relationship with God. This has been a strong connection for me since I was a teenager. I know my life has been designed with a purpose, and I travel that road with intention and feel blessed each day. This is a priority. Loving yourself is so powerful and is the second most important relationship to cultivate. This discovery is a huge gift for you. You are worthy and deserve to be loved and cherished for who you are and who you are becoming. Not every day do I feel I'm all that special. But what I do know is that there is no one like me. I'm the only one with this design, I don't have to compete with anyone, just define who I'm meant to be, and determine how I can make a difference in the world. Then go do it. Even when I don't feel like it, my life is better when I get into my game and play full out.

This is important. I like to practice *getting rid of the magic wand*. The game we often play with ourselves - the desire to wave a *magic wand* wishing we looked like someone else, acted like someone else, had better gifts and talents like someone else; and on and on. This is a no-win game. So smash your *magic wand* and start to appreciate your qualities. I have this conversation with myself often. However, the more I appreciate my own gifts and talents, the less I complain about who I'm not.

Recently, I gave an assignment to one of my clients suffering from low self-esteem, which kept her from reaching her goals and being happy. I asked her to purchase a small Post-Note pad then write on each of the 50 sheets, "I'm more than enough," then post them everywhere to see each day. At the end of the month when she checked back in, she had a smile and was excited to tell me about her possibilities. Sometimes we just have to see things physically to internalize them emotionally.

Thirdly, relationships with others give life substance and meaning. The first thing that comes to mind is "warm fuzzy" love, which of course I cherish in my long-lasting relationship with Dale. And I feel a similar love for my children and grandchildren. It's a feeling from deep in my heart. You are probably like me, having life-long friendships. My friend Sandy and I have been *Best Buds* for over 50 years. She couldn't be more of a sister to me if we'd shared the same parents. In fact this friendship was the training ground for more wonderful friendships to follow.

However, not all relationships stem from that same emotional level. Many times in the beginning it's a choice we make to care about another. And then this can be just the beginning, of a beautiful friendship. Living life this long, I've been through the Friendship and Relationship 101 Class, and know for a fact that you can create wonderful connections with others that just might grow into friendships.

Compliment freely, send thank you and appreciation notes regularly, and remember no one is just like you, so forgive them for those differences. Dale and I learned in marriage, never ever go to bed mad. Great advice from someone long ago. And remember, the more you love yourself, the more you are able to love others. If you've been around me for long, you will hear me talk about my *Balcony People*.

These are the ones that stand up and cheer you on. Often times they see things in you; gifts, talents, and qualities that you don't even know exist. They are the ones that shine the light on your greatness and stand there with you until you can believe and see it too, then go forward on your own much more powerfully. My *Balcony People* have played a strong role in my becoming who I am today. They are a cherished gift.

In my mind, I picture the people that have crossed my path and have been on the journey with me. I see it in my mind so clearly as my *life's tapestry*. I can see it so vividly, a display of colors and delicate threads. In the early years the colors of my tapestry were more pastel, and as I move forward in my life, the colors have grown into a more intense and brilliant display of beauty. Having this evidence in my mind of how important others have been in my life, and hopefully I've been in theirs, gives me a deep since of gratitude.

From this space I overflow, allowing my gratitude to turn into to contribution to make my difference in the world. This legacy I leave my family: to love others as God loves us.

THE MAGIC OF SERENDIPITY

by Jan Fowler

The world had suddenly screeched to a halt. No longer was there anything happy and wonderful to look forward to. First of all, I no longer fit in anywhere as before. Secondly, I was sad and lonely because I had just retired from my job (a huge loss) at the same time that I'd ended my marriage.

So whereas one day I was enjoying the fullness of life in my busy roles as a speech pathologist who helped recovering stroke patients learn to speak again and that of a homemaker who took pride in baking fresh apple pies, I was suddenly alone with too much time on my hands to brood. There were no more early morning meetings to rush off to, no progress reports to crank out under tight deadlines, no one at home to cook for, and no nearby grandsons who needed loving supervision after school (now that both were in high school, they were men of the world).

I'd never lived alone before. My loving children were prospering in their own careers and raising families so I had no one else to nurture but myself. At first, it felt selfish to be focused on me-me-me. But nurture myself I did once I discovered that self-*care* was not selfish, it was a necessity. And I gradually realized that living alone had unexpected perks, namely, there was no one to hold me back or whose welfare depended upon whether I succeeded or failed.

But who *was* I anyway, and what new dream could I possibly dream which was deep and wide enough to fill my empty soul? During my wonderful career as a speech pathologist I had developed a deep passion for the older population, followed by a secret desire to become an ambassador for seniors by hosting TV programs on the joys of senior living, when families are raised and the focus is on *us*. But I knew of no one who could train me in television hosting skills.

Have you ever wondered about those times when, while looking for one thing, you stumble upon something new? Favorable luck of this special nature is serendipity, which is not something you can expect to meet head on. To discover serendipity you must be searching for something *else*. And coincidentally I *was* searching for something else. I was seeking a keynote speaker for a fundraising luncheon I was sponsoring and finally located a top-notch speaker. When we met to discuss her message, I happened to also mention my need for a TV hosting coach. Her response caught me off guard. "Oh, I've done that and know the perfect trainer for you!" Can you imagine? While seeking a keynote speaker I was led to a wonderful coach. Clearly serendipity.

One day, shortly after completing hosting training at CBS in Los Angeles, I stopped to pay my bill at my local newspaper office where I fell into conversation with the editor-in-chief. He casually asked, "So what are you up to these days?" When I said I hoped to host television programs on senior life, to my surprise, he invited me to become a regular columnist on these topics for his paper.

Serendipity again. I was only looking to pay my bill, but stumbled upon an opportunity which would open new vistas for me which I could never have dreamed or imagined for my life. In time, I would become an award-winning columnist with two million readers in ten states, a speaker at senior dating expos, a television host, plus author of an award-winning book.

From emptiness and loneliness following retirement and divorce, to exciting new purpose and unimagined opportunities, I no longer had time to brood. I was helping people again and was highly gratified by readers and listeners who thanked me for inspiring and motivating them to exercise, practice good nutrition, stay active, and find new purpose in their senior years.

After a year of hosting television programs, I took time out to write *Hot Chocolate for Seniors* and go on book tour when the magic of serendipity unexpectedly crept into my life again. Since numerous retired people had approached me to organize a senior speed dating event where they could meet others, I decided to give it a try. I scheduled a classy party and bought ads in newspapers and on a radio station. And though it aroused great buzz and excitement among women, we just didn't have enough men signed up so were forced to cancel. I was very disheartened because I had disappointed so many women. Nothing favorable had resulted from my efforts; or so I thought.

So can you imagine my shock when the manager with whom I had placed ads at the radio station called to invite me to host a weekly radio program on senior living? At that moment, I felt an electric current surge throughout my body. Out of this failed speed dating project, an opportunity was born for me to host and broadcast *Senior Living at its Best*, covering inspiring guest interviews about adventure, travel, writing books, pursuing lifelong learning, fulfilling dreams, and chasing new goals in later life to 12 million listeners. What joy I've received from cards and calls from gratified listeners! *Serendipity*. Look for one thing, find something else.

The greatest lesson I ever learned was that once I learned to *expect* serendipity, it continued to reappear as a powerful force in my life again and again, and even brought me love (no kidding). While taking a dance class one ordinary Tuesday afternoon to gain information for a segment I was producing on the benefits of ballroom dancing, I met David (tall, handsome, and ready for love) and we became instant sweethearts. That "first dance" was more than eight years ago and we are still celebrating our love. Just think, while gathering material for my program, I discovered love and happiness. Serendipity applies to us all as we journey through life. As I learned to expect it, *you* can too. So I urge you to claim it, be open to it, and rejoice in it. New discoveries keep us forever young.

JAN FOWLER is an award-winning columnist, author of the prize-winning book, *Hot Chocolate for Seniors*, and the radio talk show host of *Senior Living at its Best*, broadcasting to 12 million people throughout southern California on KIK AM 1510. She received the *Golden Halo Award for Outstanding Literary Achievement* from Southern California Motion Picture Council, is founding president of Starburst Inspirations, an award-winning nonprofit corporation which supports Drug Court, and was one of ten Inland Empire women honored with a Town & Gown "Phenomenal Woman Award" for service to community. Jan has five grandchildren and lives in southern California.

JAN'S *SAVVY WOMAN* TIPS

Remain Open to Unexpected Discovery and Chance Encounters – Teach yourself to anticipate that life will surprise and delight you in magical ways, then watch how obstacles in your path tend to disappear.

Unlock Your Personal Power – Be bold and stretch your vision for your life. A powerful mind produces a powerful life so don't be afraid to go after what you want!

Never Give Up On Your Dreams or Goals – Use your imagination to pretend what those joyful outcomes will feel like when they arrive.

Take One Small Step in the Direction of Your Goal – Build momentum and often all the right people will "magically" appear just long enough to help elevate you to the next level.

Smile Often at Others – Make eye contact, and be open to new connections all day long.

Find out more about Jan at
www.JanFowler.com

I AM POSSIBLE

by Maria Serbina

The shrill ringing of the phone woke me. Who could be calling me at 2 o'clock in the morning? My first thought was something happened to my parents. After picking up the phone, a man's voice with a Chechen accent was on the other line telling me about my kids and their school route. He said I better watch them. He also mentioned money and the huge parcel of land that our company owned in Moscow. He hung up the phone. Fear was crawling all over me. My mind was racing! It was March 1994, in Magadan, Russia.

I began getting phone calls almost every week. What could I do to protect my girls and my family? I was frantically trying to find a solution. I was watching my kids like a hawk. A few months later when I was walking in downtown Moscow, a newspaper stand suddenly caught my attention. I noticed a newspaper named *Foreigner*. It must be new because I had never seen it before. I bought it. After flipping through the pages I found a very interesting article about professional immigration to Canada. This article mentioned that IT and engineering professions, in particular, were most desired there. Bingo! I found my solution.

When I told my husband and my parents about professional immigration to Canada, they started laughing at me and said, "Impossible, at least for you." I think since my horoscope sign is Taurus, I have one crazy trait in my personality. Determination. If someone challenges me with the impossible, I will make it possible.

When I made my decision, I had no clue as to how many mountains I would have to move to get our Landed Immigrant Status in Canada (Canadian Green Card). First, I decided to follow western practice by hiring an immigration lawyer. I hired a well-known law firm in Toronto that was recommended by one of my friends in Israel. They promised to provide a job offer in Canada that would help increase our chances for professional immigration. I talked to their representative in Moscow, paid a $5,000 service fee, and submitted all the paperwork. A few months later I got a phone call from the Canadian embassy. The embassy referent told me that she had our file on her table without the processing fee of $800. She continued to tell me that normally they send back files without payment right away. However, for some reason, our file had been sitting in the mailroom for two months. She said, "If you want the embassy to process the application form, you have to make a payment in the next three days before December 24, 1994." She also mentioned that the embassy only accepted U.S. dollars and foreign money orders.

My first thought was, "Impossible!" I was 5,900 kilometers, or an 8-hour flight, from Magadan to Moscow. I didn't have money to buy a ticket or pay the application processing fee. But I was on a mission to make it possible. I made it to the Canadian Embassy on December 23, 1994 with $800 in my hand. Merry Christmas!

On May 21, 1995, my family arrived at the Canadian Embassy for an interview. The moment we walked into the interview room, our immigration officer asked us why we decided to hire this particular law firm. Following our explanation, he informed us that our lawyers were arrested for fraud and money embezzlement. They collected money from hundreds of people in Russia and Israel, but never submitted their files to the embassies. The law firm embezzled more than two million dollars. He said that we were one of the eight families whose files reached them. He also mentioned that there was not a job offer in our file.

After 90 minutes of an exhausting interview, the immigration officer called his referent and said, "I have never seen so much determination to make the impossible possible. These people earned the right to live in my country, Canada."

This was only the beginning. We had to go through medical examinations, which meant we had to fly to Moscow a few times, because that was the only international medical center at that time. We had to sell our apartment in Magadan. We were required to deposit $12,000 in any bank outside of Russia, and bring proof to the embassy. To make the deposit, we took a trip to Israel. We had an incredible experience visiting Jerusalem and touching the Holy West Wall. We got our Landed Immigrant papers at the beginning of November 1995.

On January 15, 1996, my family landed at Pearson International Airport in Toronto to begin our new life in Canada. The person that met us at the airport was a relative of one of my sister's students. Even though we lived in the same town back home, we had never met before. His first question was about our legal status. When I told him we had Landed Immigrant Status, he smiled and said, "Welcome home. You will love Toronto."

It was the biggest celebration and the beginning of a new chapter in our lives. Three years later, we were granted Canadian Citizenship. In the years that followed, I helped several families relocate to Canada as professionals. It has been 20 years since I had a crazy impossible idea to leave Russia and change my life. In the beginning, I worked different jobs, cleaned houses and watched psychiatric patients at the hospitals. As of today, I have two businesses and help hundreds of people grow their business, improve their health, and stay youthful and confident.

If you asked me what drives me to help other people, my answer would be, "Other people's success, even success by an inch."

"Nothing is impossible, the word itself says 'I'm possible'!" ~ Audrey Hepburn

MARIA SERBINA, MBA, M. ENG. is an Innovative Business Strategist & Social Influence Online Expert. She holds two Master Degrees; Construction Engineering and Business Administration E-Commerce. Maria has been the proud owner of two businesses. She teaches entrepreneurs how to get more exposure and credibility, create celebrity status, and get outstanding results using social influence marketing and the power of Google+. Maria owned a successful Trade and Construction Company in Russia at the age of 27.

MARIA'S *SAVVY WOMAN* TIPS

Never, Never, Never, Ever Give Up – You can change the course, choose a different road to your goal, but never stop halfway or three feet from the goal.

Believe in Yourself – A poster in my office reads, "She believed she could and she did." If I didn't believe I could change my life drastically, I would still be in a cold town in Russia, complaining about a hard life.

Ask, Act, and You Shall Receive – A magic moment happened at the West Wall in Jerusalem. I heard a divine whisper, "You can get all your heart desires. Just ask and want it. Wish to move to Canada? Granted."

Always Build Good Relationships with People – It helps with so many situations in life and business. Plus being a good person is pretty amazing.

Don't Waste Your Time and Energy on Complaining – Life is too short. You better enjoy it.

Find out more about Maria at
www.MariaSerbina.com
www.AListWealthGift.com

LIVING YOUR DESTINY

by Nancy Ferrari

As I reflect on the chapters of my life, I cherish the blessings beginning with childhood; of the gifts of an abundance of energy; carefree days where I was free to play outside all day without fear; the simplicity of life where riding a bike was all I needed to get me to where I wanted to go; and also the gift of my voice. As this fifth decade of my life has been focused on discovering my true calling in life, it's fascinating to view my life from a different perspective, as if I was standing on the mountaintop and embracing the story of my life. Before I enlighten you with my journey, including some challenges within my life, I do want to share that my twenty-first year of life brought forth a bright shining light, who is my Dominic, the love of my life who asked me to dance, and we've been dancing for 37 years. He truly saw my bright light that radiated from within my heart for which I am eternally grateful.

As I am intentional on focusing on the positives in life, I know that my positive attitude carried me through challenges, including experiences that were lodged deep within me. I have learned that whatever we hear or say remain deep within until they surface to remind us of what needs to be released. Hearing "I'll be nobody until I become somebody" were words I never thought would surface again. Until they did. Now I can reflect on these words with neutrality, as they hold no power over me anymore since I have shifted into an empowered state of mind. I know that I am not alone in having experienced disempowering and damaging words. However, I share them now as gifts as I have learned the lessons of overcoming some emotional obstacles from childhood.

This is one of the reasons why I'm passionate about working with children and encouraging them to be in their power and soar to success.

I certainly have had my share of physical challenges, which came my way in the most unusual ways. It was only four years ago in 2010 when I started hosting my radio show, which was truly a leap of faith in my courage pool, as I never imagined I'd experience the opportunity in this lifetime. However, a little pop-up in my mind surfaced reminding me of aspirations of a career in media. I majored in journalism and communications with hopes of being a writer or reporter. I can say with authority that life has a divine plan as that was the time I met Dominic, married two years later and raised our three children.

Divine memories, and wish they didn't fly by so quickly. As our youngest child went off to college, I found myself looking in the mirror and pondering, "What is my true calling?" I decided to leave my 20 year career as a legal assistant and stepped into the unknown territory of "Nancy Who". The reference to "Nancy Who" goes back to when I was prepped for kindergarten, and as I didn't like my last name as it was riddled with vowels and seemingly a mile long, such as Finnish names are, I preferred "Nancy Who". It appears rather significant as I found myself in that "Nancy Who" phase of my life again.

As I was seeking and searching for new opportunities, this time period also coincided with my path of discovering my purpose in life and what felt authentic to me. My children told me to find an avenue where I could express myself with my voice. They would tell me that I could make a tree talk if I wanted to!

What I was discovering was myself on all levels - body, mind and spirit; and the synchronicity of them all. This is where I refer back to the health challenges that came my way soon after writing my first book *Discover the Essence of You*, branding my signature coaching program and hosting my radio show. Life truly was in the fast lane as I met so many amazing supportive and like-minded people, and enjoyed attending events to connect with even more opportunities and people to meet. All was going according to plan until the unimaginable happened, as I tripped down some stairs at an event and landed face down on the floor of an auditorium. It's rather fascinating that Claudia Cooley, one of my dear friends and my cheerleader in life, was witness to it all. That was just the beginning of many starts and stops that continued, even to this day as I recover from knee surgery. What I discovered was my passion for new healing modalities, many of which I incorporate in my practice to help others.

I also embrace my tenacious character to keep going on. There was no giving up, even though it was a fleeting thought, as Claudia asked if I was okay while sprawled on the stairs. If I can't speak, I can write; if I can't write, I can read: and if I can't walk, I can cheer others on as they soar to success. We are all one!

These are the lessons in life that I embrace as they've led me to discovering the savvy successful woman I truly am. I celebrate each day as I focus on the present moment and know that whoever or whatever shows up in my life, it is definitely for a grand purpose.

As a life coach, one of my specialties is helping people effectively overcome their obstacles, challenges, old stories that hold them back in bondage from experiencing their true calling, and I truly can say, with authority, everything happens for a reason. It's how we respond to what happens in life with the knowledge that life happens FOR me, not TO me. Nancy now knows who she is, and I embrace all my experiences for they have led me to this divine place of truth. As a wife, I'm celebrating 35 years of marriage with Dominic, and we cherish our time with our three adult children and two young grandchildren.

NANCY FERRARI is the host of *The Nancy Ferrari Show* on Talk 4 Media Network and iHeartRadio, focusing on what's right in the world, and features expert guests who make a difference. Nancy is a passionate speaker, author, and contributing writer for many online publications, including Applaud Women Magazine, sharing her messages of inspiration and living an empowered life. Nancy is a Co-Author of #1 Bestsellers *Selling With Synchronicity, Contagious Optimism* and *Sexy with No Boundaries.* Nancy is also the founder of Nancy Ferrari Media & Mentoring, providing custom designed programs based on the her signature principles within her book *Discover the Essence of You.*

NANCY'S *SAVVY WOMAN* TIPS

Embrace YOU! – There is no one else like you. Honor the gift of who you are, who you are destined to be in life and embrace each moment. Stand tall with the knowledge that you are a savvy successful woman!

You are SOMEBODY! – Honor your unique qualities as we all await to experience your brilliance. Don't let anyone tell you otherwise which is only their opinion or a reflection of themselves. Shine bright!

You MATTER! – If ever you thought that you don't make a difference in the world or that you don't matter, think again.

Yes, You CAN! – Step into your greatness. Take a leap into your courage pool to find many of us who have done so.

Cheers to Your SUCCESS!

Find out more about Nancy at
www.NancyFerrari.com

CHOOSE YOU AND BE HAPPY

by Bonnie G. Hanson

With one hand on the door and ready to walk out, I turned to observe the scene before I left. This was *not* the life I'd imagined for myself. Although I had my "white picket fence dream house", that was the only piece of my world that resembled a fairy tale. Life looked good on the outside, but inside of me it was chaos.

After another frustrating conversation with my spouse, I heard Wayne Dyer's voice in my head say, "You teach people how to treat you." What? I didn't teach anyone to treat me like this! I don't understand. I'm a good person. How could I have *taught* my family to be miserable? How could *this* be my life?

Wanting to deny it, I knew deep down that Wayne's words were true, and I was the common denominator connecting the unhappy dots. The misery I saw was a reflection of my own depression. I was grumpy and sad, tired from trying to do it all and spinning my wheels going nowhere fast. I was a *Yes* woman, wife, mother, business owner and volunteer, and I was exhausted. I had no time for myself. No energy and no boundaries. Can you relate?

Life felt like it was just happening to me, one curveball after another. What a dismal way to live, constantly striking out as a victim of circumstance. The definition of insanity is "to keep doing the same thing over and over and expecting a different result", so I finally surrendered. If I wanted things to change, I knew I must change.

This was the day I woke and realized that I am responsible for my own happiness and attitude. My choice and the lens I view the world through is completely up to me. I can live in a friendly or a hostile universe. I decided to choose to be happy in spite of what was going on around me.

I decided. Deep breath. I decided to take control and start creating my life by choice instead of simply allowing life to happen by default.

Armed with my new plan of taking full responsibility, setting boundaries and scheduling *Me* at the top of the to-do list, I was excited to learn what *freedom from the chaos* would feel like. At the same time, I was terrified of what the reactions of the outside world would be to the new *Me*.

Like any new habit, it took practice. There were times when it was a rollercoaster, because it's easy to default into what's comfortable. Our comfort zone is the menace of mediocrity and a slow and painful death. We are either growing or dying even though our lizard brains seek survival and stability. We are built for greatness!

As I chose to leave neglect and guilt behind, I created new habits and routines to expand my mind and to take proper care of myself. I practiced responding to life and to circumstances instead of being reactive. As I expanded my self-care, I liked myself more. There was less judgment and less self-criticism going on in my mind.

I learned that my thoughts are things that take root in my reality, whether they are negative or positive. From my thoughts emerge my emotions, which determine how I feel and those feelings result in my actions (or inactions) that produce my results. The compounding of my results create my situations. I use the acronym TEARS (Thoughts, Emotions, Actions, Results, Situations) and remember that I can either choose TEARS of Joy or TEARS of Sorrow. I have the ultimate say, moment by moment each and every day.

Happiness is a choice and a state of being. Do not allow your happiness to be determined by anything outside of you or by the approval or actions of others. Instead, allow your happiness to grow as a result of your choices and decisions. I changed the information I allowed into my brain by listening to uplifting or educational audios during my drive time, and by reading good books instead of watching TV. By limiting my time around negative people and attending seminars and events, I met new positive people. This continues to open the door to so many opportunities (including being asked to co-author this book).

By placing myself at the top of my to-do list, I look and feel better and have more energy from exercising and eating well. The results of increased well-being are better sleep, more patience, and less stress.

This creates more resilience when things go sideways and my self-care has created more self-confidence and increased my engagement with the people in my life. My community benefits from more meaningful contributions and my family from a happier, healthier version of me. I really feel alive!

Choosing YOU is a win-win scenario! As you allow the best version of you to shine, you give others permission to do the same. This creates a ripple of well-being in the world. Self-care is not selfish. Self-care is caring for yourself and building a solid foundation for your life. When you feel your best, you do your best! This creates an overflow of energy and desire, and you can give from that space instead of giving until depleted and resentful. A huge difference!

Are you tired? Have you stuffed shame or guilt or unhappiness to the side thinking it will go away? I can tell you that it won't. Feelings must be felt for you to move forward. I believe in you and I know that you have waited long enough. This is your time! Put yourself at the top of the to-do list. It feels good to feel good, and you absolutely deserve this! If you need help, let's connect. Together we will focus on your strengths and what's going right for you so you can fully enjoy your greatness!

"Overcome the notion that you must be regular. It robs you of the chance to be extraordinary." ~ Uta Hagen

BONNIE G. HANSON, CPC is Co-Author of four books, including the #1 Bestseller *Successonomics* with Steve Forbes. She has a proven track record of success and empowering others to advance their happiness and achievement. She is fiercely committed to guiding women to achieve happy and effective high performance lives so they can consistently live from and in their full potential and create long term, enduring fulfillment. If you are looking for a proven professional who can guide you to the results you desire, look no further! Check out her website for a free gift and to stay connected and informed about upcoming books, training and events.

BONNIE'S *SAVVY WOMAN* TIPS

Decide You are Worth it and Choose to be Happy – Be the best version of you. Love and accept yourself. Forgive yourself and others. Accept your challenges as gifts and opportunities to grow. Every choice counts!

Acknowledge the Past as Your Teacher – Accept it. Move forward. You are enough! Every moment is a new beginning. Focus on possibilities. Make a plan. Go for it! Expand. Make mistakes. Play! Enjoy the journey!

Choose Extreme Self-Care – Eat and sleep well. Breathe. Drink water. Make time for quiet. Reflect. Journal. Read. Use positive self-talk. Be good to yourself. Live! Love! Laugh! Celebrate!

Feel Your Emotions – All of them. The longer you wait, the longer it hurts. Risk. Be vulnerable. Trust yourself. Follow your intuition. Be brave. You know what to do. You are unstoppable!

Associate with Positive People that Love & Accept You – This is not negotiable. Engage fully. Create deep relationships. Bring the joy!

Find out more about Bonnie at
www.BonnieGHanson.com
www.WealthMindsetMentor.com

LIVING A LIFE OF VALUE AND MEANING

by Heather Pich

Four years ago I decided to end a 25-year relationship that included almost 23 years of marriage, three children and a long road of infertility. It was one of the hardest life experiences I've had to walk through. When I married, I truly believed it would be for life. I pictured the rocking chair, the grandchildren, and the peace of mind of having family surround me. However, my marriage was a rocky road.

With differences in our personalities, and not understanding where one another came from, my husband and I battled mentally, and we battled a lot. We began counseling when our children were babies - the twins were one and our son was almost three - and we continued to work on our relationship for 15 years. In February of 2008, I said I wanted a divorce. He said he wanted to continue to try, and we worked on it for two more years. At that time, I was putting a lot into my business, most likely to dull the pain. My business was on fire, I was leading a team; writing classes, training and selling. 2010 was a big year for awards. A class I had written and taught to over 3,000 women across the country was featured in *Empowering Women Magazine*.

The demise of my marriage happened later that Fall. I found the courage to walk out with three teens (the twins were 14 years old and our son was 15). The last four and a half years have been a rough road that included three moves. I shut down emotionally for the first year, walking through an emotional fog. I was raising three emotional teens almost all on my own, dealing with the feelings they were having from the divorce. I was also running my business. In between all of this, my mother passed away unexpectedly (from a fall and brain surgery), and it all took a huge toll on me. Alone, I cried myself to sleep almost every night and prayed often.

What has gotten me through? My faith. I would be nothing without the love of God in my life - walking me through the pain, giving me hope and encouragement. I was afraid, but kept moving forward. I worked my business and tried to be there for my children. In the first 18 months I didn't date. Meanwhile, through all of this, I turned one of the classes I wrote into a book, due to all the amazing feedback I had gotten from strangers who had taken my class. I then sat on it for almost two years.

I began dating someone in December 2013, and it was to be casual. He was planning on traveling the world and taking a sabbatical in about six months and was upfront about it. We found we had an amazing connection. But through this six-month period of dating, I learned another valuable lesson. I learned that I was a liar. I lied to myself and I lied to him. I said I was ok with a casual relationship. Casual dating, no commitment. But as we spent time together and got more involved, feelings became entangled. He said he loved me, but was holding back because he knew he had to leave. In the end it was hard to let go, and the heartache was excruciating. I learned that I could love again. I hadn't realized how far I had let myself fall until I had to let him go. I called it off at the end of May 2014, and was extremely sad and felt let down.

I began looking into myself again as I always do in times of trial, and asked myself the question I always ask. "What was the lesson to be learned here?" I learned that I wasn't to lie to myself or to the person I was dating. I am not ok with casual. I am a relationship girl. I need to state what I want from the beginning and stand by what I want, and how I feel. If that means the person I am with is not on the same path as me, then I need to walk away before it gets too deep. Lesson learned.

I decided to go back to work in the corporate world and found a company that was into professional growth, personal awareness and development. The company was looking for a presenter, trainer and salesperson, and asked me to interview for them. I truly believe I was put with this company for a reason. It fit so well with what I was trying to accomplish for myself. It has been on an amazing uplifting journey to become a higher conscious thinker, and really understand how our thoughts effect our actions that we take every day.

At the end of May 2014, I began looking at my book again. I sat myself down and walked myself through the mindset I was having on this book. Why I wasn't I moving forward? I realized I was letting fear, doubt, and worry about what others would think dictate why I hadn't released it. The training and workshops on mindset that I had been doing in my corporate job helped me realize that I could either sit in fear and do nothing (as I had been); or I could sit in fear and move forward anyway, and see where it went. Even if it bombed I would still win because I would have faced my fear and learned a lesson in moving on and pushing through.

I hired a publisher, created a website, and joined a great professional like-minded team of entrepreneurs and professionals. This group became my support system. On October 1, 2014, my book launched on Amazon. This team of professionals, with friends and family, rallied around me and took my book to #1 bestseller in its main category, and bestseller in 11 other categories. I couldn't have been more surprised, humbled and thrilled all at the same time.

How do I celebrate all the beauty that has come into my life, in these different events and people that I have met? By reaching out and giving back to others. I try to serve those I have met and connect them with whomever I can to enhance their business. I have been called *the connector*. I have found that the more I reach out to help others, inspire and connect them with others that may help them, the more joy I feel. There is a saying by Zig Ziglar "The more people you help get where they want to go, the more you will get where you want to go." I believe that.

HEATHER PICH is the #1 Bestselling Author of *Bookings When You Have No Bookings: A Guide to Keeping Your Sales Calendar Full* and Co-Author of *Driving Ambitions*, #1 Bestselling Audiobook/CD. She's a Mentor and Trainer for Productive Learning, a professional growth company in Capistrano Beach, CA. She built a million dollar team, earning numerous awards for sales, leadership and sponsorships. Highlighted in *Empowering Women Magazine* in 2010, she wrote several training classes for the direct sales industry, training at national conventions for 3000+ entrepreneurs. Heather educates on MINDSET in her workshops *Does Your Thinking Limit Your Success* and *Maximizing Your Potential*.

HEATHER'S *SAVVY WOMAN* TIPS

Know Who You Are – Know what you want and be authentic with yourself. Don't lie to yourself or others about what you want.

Understand Your Mindset – We tell ourselves stories and assumptions every day that many times aren't true, but hold us back from taking action toward the successes we want.

Have a True Intention – Where do you want to go with your life? List your top 5 morals and values.

Have a Servant's Heart – Are you serving others and showing you care first before you try to sell yourself to others? People want to work with people that they know truly care about them.

Start Your Day with Your Maker – Be grateful for what you have. Write your 555's down every day. 5 minutes, 5 people you are grateful for, 5 things you are grateful for. Meditate on it and watch your world soar.

Find out more about Heather at
www.ProductiveLearning.com
www.InstantlyBooked.com

THE MIRACLE OF MANIFESTING IMPOSSIBLE

by Irina Baker

The day was a typical day in Kazan, Russia. My good friend and I were riding a bus to our university. It was a normal, overcrowded bus that we had just stormed on to board; too many people, not enough buses. We all had to get to our destinations. The strongest and the angriest would survive, every day, literally.

My friend and I were squashed like sardines in a can, breathless. I suddenly exclaimed to my her, "Watch my word! The day will come and I will have my own car. I won't use public transportation ever again." My friend answered in a calm voice, "I am fine. I am ok with public transportation."

I knew that I had declared something that was not even possible. When I was growing up, women couldn't own cars. Life was difficult, and neither money nor cars were easily available. I completely forgot about this episode until many years later.

Life in Russia was hard; day-to-day survival for many people. We Russians had to have connections to buy clothes. At one point, I had to wrap my feet in plastic bags because my boots had holes. I couldn't buy new boots, not even if I had money. Boots were simply not available to buy! Material difficulties were normal for the whole country. We had to have connections to buy food, and at one time, we lived through small monthly food rations. In addition, my girlfriends and I couldn't find good relationships and lived in fear, often viewed as prey to young men.

So, I decided that Russian life was not for me. People leave behind their families, friends, and everything that is dear to them so that they can have a much better life. Some of these people often automatically assume that if you just touch American soil, you become rich by default.

My hopes were simple. I wanted to have a good relationship and career, and live happily ever after in a rich promised land where everything is great and easy.

I arrived in Florida and instantly felt at home. I found myself in paradise and couldn't absorb enough of its lush, tropical beauty. I celebrated. All my dreams of a better life have come true and my hard life was over. Finally, I had a grand time! I thought I had arrived! Time passed and gradually, everything started going downhill. I was doing my best to assimilate with the American culture and the new lifestyle. The relationship I was in started taking a bad turn. Within a year, I didn't want to live in America anymore, nor did I want to return to Russia. All I wanted was to get on a transatlantic plane. And I hoped that the plane would crash with me on board in the middle of an ocean. I didn't know what to do or where to find the solution to my internal emotional suffering. Fortunately, the miraculous moment was approaching fast, and I had no idea that my life would never be the same.

One memorable day, I was sitting in my home office typing something on the computer, very focused and quiet. Suddenly, a thousand light bulbs turned on inside my head. The light was powerful and overwhelming. A sudden, very deep subconscious realization came up to the surface. "You are responsible for everything in your life, good and bad. You are responsible for all your broken relationships as well."

I had no idea what was happening, but I responded with a decisive, "I will find out what inside of me is holding me back, and I will change it." Little did I know what powerful intent I had created, and the spiritual forces began to flow. My spiritual awakening took place in 1996. Since that profound moment, I have devoted my life to self-healing and awareness growing. Along the way over the years, I helped numerous men and women do the same. Since then I realized that there is nothing impossible in our dreams. Dreams are placed in our hearts for a reason!

Unconsciously, by declaring to my friend on the bus, "One day I will have my own car," I set up a powerful intent to change my miserable life of material and emotional survival. Then, without even understanding what I was doing, I took inspired actions and turned my intent into reality. Moving to America for me was like moving to the moon. Mission Impossible. Yet, I have been living in America since 1995. I have already driven several brand new cars and consequently, I haven't used public transportation since then. My Russian friend still lives in Russia, doesn't have a car, and uses buses every day. But she is ok with all that. "To each its own," as they say.

Then I had a second major realization. By leaving Russia and having come to the other side of the earth, I truly believed that my life would change all by itself. What I had learned was that I couldn't run away from myself, or my internal energy frequency. I brought Russia to America inside of me, and the Russian survival was still actively creating my life.

To have a better life, I had to increase my energy vibration. That is exactly what I have accomplished, and what I celebrate now. The increase of my frequency changed my personality, my destiny, my life in all respects, and that is what I have been helping people with. Increasing personal frequency by removing the internal darkness, and replacing it with the bright spiritual light; thus making a quantum leap in shifting awareness onto a much higher level when you know how to easily manifest good things, and how to confidently solve your challenges. When you stop letting your ego have control, you allow yourself to flow in a river of life, being fully connected with the Divine, receiving Divine Guidance and manifesting your heart's desires. Yes, my path was extremely difficult, but it brought me to the life and the spiritual level of awareness I enjoy now. For that, I am eternally grateful.

IRINA BAKER M.A., C.H. is The Total Mind-Set Makeover Mentor and Author of three books. Irina teachers entrepreneurs the innovative Mirror™ system to move from being stuck and functioning by default to be in the flow by using the knowledge based on awareness. Irina holds three Master's degrees and has 20 years of experience.

IRINA'S *SAVVY WOMAN* TIPS

Don't Blame the Mirror for Your Face – The world you see is a reflection of you.

Impossible Big Dream – It is in your heart for a reason. You always have two choices: ignore it and live your life as you know it now, or take a risk and go after your heart's desire.

Set Serious Endeavors with Intent – Declare it out loud. "I intend to graduate from the college." "I intend to find my dream job."

Don't Do It Alone – Ask your trusted Higher Power to help you. "If you don't ask, you don't gain."

Internal Preparation – Achieving any dream ALWAYS starts inside. Set the expectation of what you want and create a vision.

Find out more about Irina at
www.IrinaBaker.com
www.FreeGiftFromIrina.com
www.DreamManifestingFormula.com

FOCUS ON THE SUCCESS OF OTHERS

by Victoria Schumacher

As a single mother for over ten years, I raised my daughter, Veronica. This was especially challenging for me since Veronica lived with me full time due to her father living on the other side of the country. I worked very long hours as a school district administrator as I strove to be a great mother.

While I did not know another woman who faced similar challenges who could serve as a role model, I believed that I had the capacity to balance my aspirations for career and motherhood. This belief and my faith in God helped me in preparing Veronica for a life of great success. It was hard to find time to build friendships with the parents of my daughter's friends, since I was so busy buying food, cooking, cleaning and doing laundry during my limited time away from work. I continually explored how Veronica and I could participate in a healthy community of families and neighbors, while having so much on my plate.

In an effort to minimize the tasks I faced at home, I took many concrete steps with limited resources available to me. For example, I hired a cleaning lady who came once a month. I found a dry cleaning business that picked up and delivered my clothing from our apartment each week. I washed and hung our clothing to dry inside of our apartment, which eliminated the time needed to wait for a dryer's drying cycle. I purchased prepared food once a week so that Veronica and I could heat up food instead of cooking.

As a result of this approach in minimizing the work I faced at home, Veronica was able to focus on her homework, take a nap, and prepare her own dinner. Each evening, I was able to spend at least an hour in conversation with my daughter during our three-mile walk after I returned home from work. We became friends with our neighbors and shopkeepers during these walks. On occasion, we even stopped for ice cream.

When we returned home from our walks, I was available to help Veronica prepare for her exams, if she requested help. She would work late into the night on her homework after I went to sleep. While she did not have transportation available for afterschool enrichment activities, since I did not arrive home until approximately 6:30 p.m. each night, we enjoyed many weekend activities. For example, Veronica participated in debate tournaments during the weekends. Together, we explored local bookstores, saw films at independent movie theaters, and attended a number of theatrical performances.

For three summers during high school, Veronica traveled in other parents' cars, by metro and by bus from our home in Pasadena to the University of California, Los Angeles, in order to develop mathematics games. Through research studies with my work in education, I was able to engage with colleagues regarding a national research endeavor that included my daughter and her friends. Even though game development was not Veronica's greatest area of interest, she and I realized that it was valuable for her to contribute to this research opportunity since Veronica loved to conduct research and write.

In March of Veronica's senior year of high school, she received an offer to attend Harvard College. We celebrated her success with family and friends during a special dinner on the day of her high school graduation. On my own, I celebrate my success as a mother by thanking God for motivating me to sustain my efforts through many challenging years. I continue to pray for the strength and wisdom to serve my daughter, my family, the students in my school district, and my colleagues in ways that help everyone thrive.

VICTORIA SCHUMACHER, Ph.D., serves as the Superintendent of Coast Unified School District. In California, she has served as a teacher, an assistant principal, a principal, a director of assessment and special projects, and an assistant superintendent of curriculum and instruction. Victoria earned her B.A. in music and M.A. in education at the University of California, Berkeley. She earned her Ph.D. in education at the University of California, Los Angeles. Victoria thrived in her career while supporting her daughter in realizing her dream of attending Harvard College.

VICTORIA'S *SAVVY WOMAN* TIPS

Focus on the Success of Others – This reflects your own success.

Love Unique Contributions – Each person makes them, even if he or she is has a challenging personality.

Continually Assess Your Priorities – It is important to remain nimble to adjust as needed.

Focus on Building a Healthy Family System and Work Organization – Take steps to minimize chaos and politics.

High Priority – Maintain your own health.

Find out more about Victoria at
www.Coastusd.org

ABOUT CLAUDIA COOLEY

Claudia Cooley is on a mission to inspire others to live their most empowered life. That's exactly why she founded Claudia Cooley, Inc., a Professional Success and Life Enrichment company, where for over three decades she's provided workshops, programs and products designed to build your life and business with momentum and fulfillment. Always keeping your bottom line in mind, her focus is to expand and enrich all areas of your life: Your Health, Wealth, Relationships, Legacy, and Branding (how the world sees you). It's all about "Building Your Success Synergy."

As an accomplished Success Mentor and Mind Shift Business Coach, Claudia shares dynamic methods to empower men and women to enhance and express their unique gifts, talents, vision and dreams to bring more happiness, fulfillment, and real significance to their lives. A vibrant speaker with a slightly humorous style, Claudia draws upon her innate talents as an inspiring communicator, delivering high-energy presentations, trainings and workshops to audiences everywhere. Her clients include entrepreneurs, authors, business leaders, and individuals committed to living a life they love – one that allows them to live personal excellence and to give to others powerfully.

Claudia is the #1 Bestselling Author of *The 7 Mind Shifts to Ignite Your Success*, *From Dud to Stud: Revving up for Success,* and *Savvy Women Revving Up For Success: Women Making a Difference in the World Today*; She's the Host /Producer of *Rev Up For Success* Radio show.

CLAUDIA'S *SAVVY WOMAN* TIPS

Aspire – Always reach for your personal and unique A+.

Greatness is in You – Never, ever settle for second best.

Journal – Spend quiet time every day with yourself.

Grateful – Have an attitude of gratitude.

Thank You – Write and send 3 notes to people every day: thank you, I appreciate you, or I'm proud of you. And yes, mail with a stamp.

Have a Huge Dream – Create a vision board.

Stay Connected – Check in with friends regularly.

Have Fun – Enjoy Freedom in everything you do.

Enjoy Vibrancy and Vitality at Any Age – Eat Healthy, get lots of sleep, engage in movement.

Find out more about Claudia at
www.ClaudiaCooley.com
www.facebook.com/ClaudiaCooleyInc

BOOKS FROM
CLAUDIA COOLEY

From Dud to Stud
Revving Up for Success

Accelerate your success and enjoy the ride.
It's time to put the pedal to the metal.
Your mountain top is waiting for you!

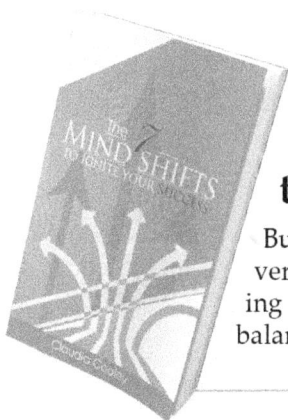

The 7 Mind Shifts
to Ignite Your Success

Building your life on your own terms is a
very exciting journey. The keys for designing a life that you love are found in creating
balance in all areas of your life.

Savvy Women
Revving Up for Success
Women Making a Difference in the
World Today

Live life full out as you enjoy your journey to
success. Discover your gifts by seeing the
greatness in yourself and paying it forward,
shining your light for others to follow.

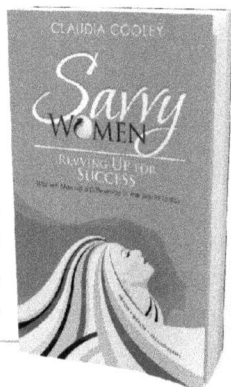

Available Fall 2015 –
Revving Up for Success
with a Winning Image